LITERARY THEORY
FOR BEGINNERS®

BY
MARY KLAGES

ILLUSTRATED BY
FRANK REYNOSO

FOREWORD BY
BILL BROWN

FOR BEGINNERS®

For Beginners LLC
30 Main Street
Suite 303
Danbury, CT 06810 USA
www.forbeginnersbooks.com

A For Beginners® Documentary Comic Book
Copyright © 2017

Cataloging-in-Publication information is available from the Library of Congress.

ISBN-13 # 978-1-939994-60-8 Trade

Manufactured in the United States of America

For Beginners® and Beginners Documentary Comic Books® are published by For Beginners LLC.

First Edition

10 9 8 7 6 5 4 3 2 1

To all the CU English majors who have taught me Literary Theory

Contents

FOREWORD
by Bill Brown

Literary theory is a prompt. It is a provocation to think more intensely about literature: about what it is, how it works, what effect it can have—on you, on me. No less, literary theory provides an analytical frame through which to discover, within a literary text, the dynamics that animate individual subjects, say, or specific cultures. It is a mode of reading. There are many theories, often conflicting, that make up the thing called *literary theory*. To gain some familiarity with them is, most fundamentally, to appreciate the range of complexities that works of literature disclose and to amplify your awareness of what a complex phenomenon literature is.

When you sit down to think about a Shakespeare play, do you think about it as the expression of its historical moment (addressing the politics of the Stuart monarchy, say); as the investigation of a trans-historical human emotion (love, jealousy, anger, sadness); as an inquiry into gender relations; as a philosophical examination (of ethical responsibility); as a self-reflexive meditation (about theater); or as a scrutiny of language itself (the power of metaphor)? Insofar as theory is a way of looking at things (*thereos* is the observer or spectator), you are a theorist whether you know it or not. Learning something about literary theory, then, also means learning something about your own habits of mind and being able to describe those habits more precisely. So, too, it means having those habits disrupted, finding yourself productively dislodged from one or another reading routine.

Literary theory has also become recognized as a body of thought that stretches from the ancient to the contemporary worlds. It became a particularly energetic and contested body of thought in the last decades of the 20th century, when it challenged many institutional (and institutionalized) routines of appreciating and understanding great works of literature. So, too, it thwarted an aspiration—shared by linguistics and cybernetics—to gain full command of apprehending the production of meaning and the process of communication. The so-called culture wars of the 1980s changed the literary canon and expanded the notion of literature itself; those conflicts were funded in part by theory's revolution against unnoticed conformities and complacencies.

Just as literary theory was informed by a wide range of radical thought—the work of Karl Marx, Friedrich Nietzsche, and Sigmund Freud, most obviously—likewise it was enlivened by avant-garde writing—the work of such figures as Antonin Artaud, Georges Bataille, and Paul Celan. Indeed, so-called French Theory often feels like the perpetuation of the avant-garde in a different mode even as it redevelops the social politics of the 1960s within a philosophical register. Gilles Deleuze and Félix Guattari make clear how much they learned from the likes of Kafka, Henry Miller, and William Burroughs. Hélène Cixous, famous as a literary critic, is also famous as a playwright and a poet. And like much of the avant-garde, theorists often want to disrupt more than familiar habits of reading, of writing history, or of understanding how human subjects are shaped. They want to change the world.

That desire helps to explain how *literary theory* morphs into a body of thought (*cultural theory* or simply *theory*) that sets its sight both within and beyond literature. On the one hand, the Russian formalists of the first decade of the 20th century developed focused accounts of the way narratives are constructed (within a field that became known as *narratology*); a German emphasis on the experience of literature led to *reader-response criticism*; and *poetics* continues to inquire into questions of style and figurative language. On the other hand, for feminist theory, queer theory, and postcolonial theory, for instance, the focus expands from the text to the social fabric. Unsurprisingly, then, literary theory has had an impact on many fields: anthropology, history, political science, legal studies. That impact derives not least from theory's concern with *difference*—both the difference *between* (classes, genders, cultures) and the difference *within* (including the difference within a single psyche, a single statement, a single word).

Of course, there are readers of literature who have happily ignored theory, as have more than a few literary critics. Indeed there have been critics who write "against theory," and others who declare the "end of theory" and the "death of theory." It turns out, though, that literary theory does not die so easily. That is because it has been internalized: theory has left a lasting impact on the way that literature is taught, providing an expanded tool kit for taking texts apart and putting them back together again. It's also because literary theory is all but inseparable from particular social movements, above all feminism. And it's because just when some theories start to fade others emerge: *affect theory, thing theory, assemblage theory*. Theory may provide you with answers to questions you've already had. More likely it will provide you with new questions. These are not simply questions with which you can now interrogate a play of Shakespeare's more energetically. They are questions that enable you to think differently about literature and language, society and culture—the world we live in . . . the world as it is, and about the world as it might yet be.

Mary Klages has done a remarkable job of distilling and demystifying the body of thought, forms of inquiry, and shifting perspectives of literary theory from the ancient to the contemporary. Her skills as a teacher, her sense of humor, and her passion for the subject are sure to draw you in and help you reach new levels of insight and appreciation for literature and reading itself.

Bill Brown *is the Karla Scherer Distinguished Professor of American Culture at the University of Chicago. He teaches in the Department of English and the Department of Visual Culture, and is the author, most recently, of* Other Things *(2015). He has served as co-editor of* Critical Inquiry *since 1993.*

Dear Reader,

This is a book about Literary Theory. It comes out of a course I teach in the English Department at the University of Colorado at Boulder called "Introduction to Literary Theory."

So what is "Literary Theory"? Well, that's what the book is about, so you'll have to read more than this Introduction to find out.

In my class—which is required for English majors—I start off with a bad joke. "If you are an astronomer," I say, "you can spend your life asking the question 'Is there life on other planets?' If you are an engineer, you can spend your life asking 'What's the best way to build this?' And if you are an English major, you can spend the rest of your life asking 'You want fries with that?'"

Groan.

But seriously—what kinds of questions do we ask when we study literature?

Notice I said "study," not just "read." Literary Theory doesn't have a whole lot of "literature" in it—Lit Theory talks about how we think about literature, not just how we read it. Or, as one student put it,

> *"I used to love literature. And then you made me*
> *think about it."*

So be warned.

Like science, the study of literature has two components: an object of study (what you look at) and a methodology (how you look at the object).

We have at least an intuitive idea of what our object of study is—it's literature! It's a literary text! But HOW do we look at that object? What's our mode of investigation? Our methodology? What kind of questions are we asking?

I ask my students this on the first day of class. Their answers tend to focus on two dimensions of literary study: frameworks of interpretation, and ideas about the social functions of literature.

The majority of my students agree that the two most-asked literary questions are ...

What does this MEAN?
What does this REALLY mean?
What is the deeper meaning, the hidden meaning,
the symbolic meaning?
Are all meanings present in the text?
Did the author intend all these meanings?
Are all meanings equally valid?

And the second-most asked literary question is ...

What does this DO?
Why is literature important?
What effect does literature have on the reader?
How does literature reflect history, culture,
diversity?
How can literature be a force for social change?
What would the world lose if we didn't have
literature?

Those two major questions sum up my approach to Literary Theory in this book. The first half talks about ways to think about how literature makes meaning. The second half talks about ways to think about what literature does.

You're just going to have to read it if you want to know more.

Sincerely,

The Author

Chapter 1
HUMANIST LITERARY THEORY
(and Other Old-Fashioned Topics)

Let's start with a quick overview of the past 2,000 years of literary theory.

We'll begin at the foundations of Western culture: the Greeks. Both Plato and Aristotle thought that literature (lyric and dramatic poetry and drama, no novels yet!) should be MIMETIC—a poem is a copy, representation, or imitation of something that exists in nature. By this logic, a good poem would be a poem that is accurate in copying nature.

For Plato, this was a problem. Plato argued that the natural world is itself only a copy of an ideal world of forms that exists in the abstract. Since only the ideal/eternal Forms can be perfect, the natural world is flawed and imperfect. A poem, then, is a copy of a copy, so doubly flawed. Thus, Plato banned poets from his Republic, because they told lies.

Plato

3

Aristotle wasn't quite so stern. His writings focus on the natural world (rather than abstract forms) in order to describe and classify all phenomena in it. So Aristotle didn't worry about mimesis so much. He believed that poetry and art could imitate the natural world, but that they add something in doing so—they make real world happenings have MEANING for audiences. Aristotle's idea is that art serves as supplement to the real world; it's a way of representing the real world that helps audiences better understand it.

The emphasis on MIMESIS raised problems, as you might see. Can a poet write about things not found in nature? What about imagination? Is nature "out there" for us to copy, or do we create "nature" in the act of writing about it?

Plato and Aristotle were the main voices in lit theory until the early modern age (Renaissance and after). In the 17th century, English philosopher John Locke asserted that the mind is a tabula rasa, or blank slate, until sensory perception puts experiences into our brains, which we then sort and collect and make sense of. Nothing exists in our minds, Locke maintained, except what comes through that sensory perception (and the secondary processes of ordering and drawing conclusions from it—which form consciousness). For literature, this meant that writers should focus on descriptions of the external world, trying to use words to replace sensory perceptions to fill up a mind seen as passive, like a sponge. Good literature was that which put good thoughts into your head.

The function of literature, from this perspective, is DIDACTIC—literature should tell you how to think correctly about people and things and the world in general. "Good" literature tells you good things; bad literature tells you bad,

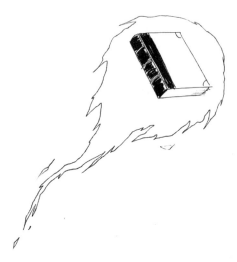

wrong, immoral things.

In the 18th century, philosophers began to refigure their concepts of the human mind, moving away from Locke's tabula rasa to the idea that the mind actively shapes and interprets sense data. Rather, they posited a "constitutive imagination," or the mind's ability to create ideas whose whole is greater than the sum of their parts. A poem, then, didn't have to be a copy of nature, or of sense impressions— poets could make things up, imagine them, and then write down what they imagined.

As you might agree, this was a great development for literature and art! The purpose of art as imitating nature gave way to the idea of art as CREATION—and thus of the artist as a kind of God.

This gave rise, by the end of the 18th century, to the Romantic era and the idea that literature is an expression of an inner truth, a "deeper meaning." The function of literature, in the Romantic view, is to be EXPRESSIVE of the complexity of the artist's inner feelings and thoughts, which could not be expressed any other way.

Good literature, though, was not just expressive—the author spilling his guts/vomiting on the page. It also had to be AFFECTIVE. It had to move the reader, get the reader to feel powerful emotions aroused by the author's words. Aristotle had articulated this function of literature in his discussion of *catharsis* (emotional purging) in tragedy.

The expressive and affective aspects of literature formed the basis for most literary study from the Romantic era until the last decades of the 20th century. This is what we call **humanist literary theory.**

Expressive and affective literary theory put new emphasis on the Author as creator—it's MY inner experience I have to express. This model also placed new emphasis on the Reader as the recipient of the author's creative genius and tortured emotions. This, too, contributed to the attention paid to "what literature does."

Among the things a poem could do for, or give to, a reader:

- moral improvement
- knowledge/education of fact and history
- pleasure
- psychological insight
- catharsis
- an approach to the sublime (God, the divine, the inexpressible/unsayable)
- aesthetic appreciation

Each of these attributes or benefits gave rise to a branch of literary criticism and theory, including a method for evaluating what literature is good or great, and what is crap.

One other notable method developed in the early 20th century in Anglo American literary thought: FORMALISM, or what was then called New Criticism. Formalism rejected any analysis of the author or the reader, any expressive or affective notions of the function of literature. For formalists, a literary work is words on a page, nothing else. The job of the literature student or literary critic, they maintained, is to understand how the words on a page create meaning (real meaning, deeper meaning) without reference to anything outside the text. Formalism considered itself the only

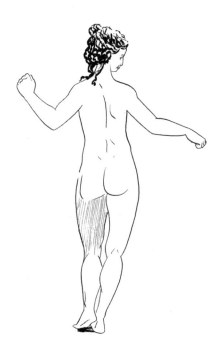

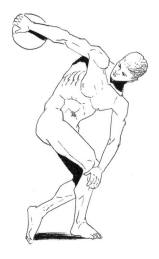

objective way of viewing a literary text; hence it became the main method taught by English departments. Academic pursuits, it was believed, should be modeled on the sciences; they should be objective, measurable, and fully explicable. Literary studies are often in danger of being called "subjective," because they are based on personal taste or individual interpretation, rather than on objective fact.

To sum up: The humanist model presupposes that great literature is...

- a unique creation coming from the most profound inner experiences of an author
- a creation that can move readers emotionally and intellectually, to get them to understand themselves better

- a means of raising consciousness, for getting readers to think about themselves and the world differently
- a work that "withstands the test of time"— that speaks to all periods of history and all cultures because it addresses ideas and events common to all people at all times in all cultures
- an expression of "universal human truth" unaffected by history, ethnicity, geography, or anything else external to the text. The assumption is that human nature is unchanging, that people are pretty much the same everywhere, in all ages and all cultures, and that "we" all share something by virtue of our common humanity.

The humanist ideal of "great" literature also supports the idea of an individual "self" to which great literature speaks—the inner truths that make us who we are, our essential self. Even though all humans are essentially the same, sharing a common humanity, each one of us (in Western culture, anyway) is a unique individual, like no one else who has ever existed.

Now forget all that.

Chapter 2
STRUCTURALISM

The formalist method insists that a text makes its own meaning, without reference to the reader, the author, the morality, or the external world (or history or cultural formation of any kind). What you do in analyzing a text is "close reading"—looking at each word, phrase, sentence, or other element and deciding how that element contributes to the unified meaning of the whole piece. Such close reading is still one of the basic skills of reading literature; no interpretation of a text can be valid without evidence from the text to support it.

The quest for textual evidence to support an argument about a literary text may sound more like science than English. The critics who developed formalism in England and the United States in the 1940s were trying to make literary criticism more scientific, to take it out of the realm of mere personal responses. They wanted a more scientific or objective approach to reading literature because

science was considered the hallmark of true knowledge.

This may strike some of us as disappointing. What we find valuable in literature, the reasons why we study it, have more to do with subjective responses than objective analysis. We love literature because it speaks to us—a great literary work is one that "withstands the test of time" and that resonates with us personally and affectively even though it was written hundreds of years ago. Within the humanist model of literature, what is valuable to us in lit is that it expresses universal human truths, ideas about the mind, the soul, about life and death, about youth, age, and experiences that are common to all people in every time and culture.

But at the end of the last chapter, I told you to forget all that.

When we talk about "literary theory," we're talking about a development that didn't really begin until the second half of the 20th century, when the humanist approach—the idea that great literature can make you a better human being (more compassionate, more understanding)—seemed inadequate in the face of the Holocaust and the atom bomb. Literary theory evolved, in part, from a rejection of humanist ideas about literature and a turn toward other ways of thinking about what literature does and how it makes meaning.

Structuralism is one of those ways. We're starting with structuralism because a lot of the theories in this book follow from structuralist ideas—which is why they are called **post-structuralist** theories.

Structuralism is a way of thinking about the world that seeks out the basic units of any structure or system. In this sense, it's like science, which posits the atom as the basic unit of which all matter is composed. Structuralists look at the interrelation between such basic units and the rules that govern how those units can combine. In science, the units are atoms, and the rules for combining them is what we call "chemistry."

So, think about Tinkertoys. The basic units are plastic rods and wheels with holes; the rule for combining them is that rods go into holes. That's the structure of Tinkertoys— everything you can make out of them (a building, a race car, a windmill) is made by using the units according to the rules. Structuralist analysis isn't interested in what you build, only in how the system of Tinkertoys allows you to build by using the units according to the rules.

Structuralism looks only at the structure of something, not at the content.

How does this work in literary theory? Well, what's the basic "unit" of a piece of literature? Right, a *word!* And what do we call the rules for putting words together to make meaning? Right, *grammar!* So structuralist literary theory looks not at any literary text as a whole, but at the basic units and rules that create the text, that create what we call "meaning."

Structuralist Linguistics

Structuralism is a very useful mode of analysis in a lot of disciplines, including economics, anthropology, religious studies, psychology, and literature. The version of structuralism we're looking at here comes from linguistics; it examines the structure of language itself. According to a structuralist examination of English, for example, the 31 phonemes that make all the sounds that combine to form any word in English are the units, and grammar is the set of rules that dictate how these words can be put together to make sense. The rules of grammar are different in every language, but the structure is the same in all languages: words are put together within a grammatical system to make meaning.

Have you ever played the word game Mad Libs? Here's an example. (Do you recognize the passage?)

14

Infinitive verb or not *infinitive verb;* that is the *noun.*
Whether it is *comparative adjective* in the mind to *verb*
the *plural noun* and *plural noun* of *adjective* fortune,
Or to take *plural body part* against a *noun* of troubles
And by opposing, *verb* them —

Mad Libs work because you can plug any unit, any word, into the place where the rules of grammar call for a noun, a verb, or another part of speech, and the passage still makes "sense"—even if it turns out silly. (That's the fun part.)

Let's see how it works for a simple narrative. Here are three characters: a stepmother, a princess, and a handsome prince. And let's say these are the rules: stepmothers are evil, princesses are oppressed, and princes rescue and marry princesses. This pattern fits the fairy tales of Cinderella and Snow White, and just about every Disney movie ever made. Whatever details you add, the basic structure (units and rules) of the story stay the same. Those basic, fixed elements are exactly what a structuralist analysis of literature, or myth, or any other form of narrative, examines.

Structuralism posits that the underlying structures which organize units and rules into meaningful systems come from the human mind itself, as a way of processing

overwhelming amounts of information and creating order. The human mind takes in a chaos of information and sorts it into structures in order to make sense of it all. For structuralists, the world we perceive is created by our mind's ability to make structure out of chaos, rather than something that exists outside our mind and enters into it through the senses.

Structuralism, as a science of humankind, works to understand the structures that underlie everything people do, think, feel, and perceive. Every human culture has systems that can be analyzed structurally: a kinship system, a language system, a government system, and an exchange system, for example, all follow the pattern that units follow rules.

In this sense, strangely enough, structuralism isn't far away from humanism—both seek out human universals, things that have always been true regardless of time, place, or belief.

So let's look at how language and meaning work from a structuralist perspective.

To begin with, a structure has to be "whole." Let's use the Tinkertoys again as an example. The Tinkertoy set consists of a system of units put together according to rules; this system functions as a whole, not just a collection of independent parts. You can't do much with just one rod or just one wheel—you need everything in the set in order to build something.

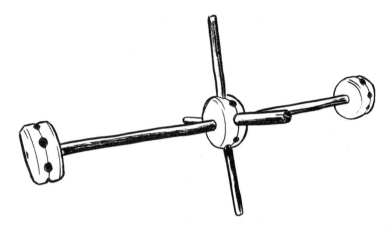

Language, as a structure, has the same property of wholeness: we need all the words in our vocabulary in order to create whatever sentences we want. If we only had one or two words, we couldn't say much.

A structure has to be able to incorporate new elements. With Tinkertoys, I can add other rods or wheels without changing the rule that rods go into holes. I could even add a plastic dinosaur if it had a tail that fit into a wheel hole!

Language is being transformed all the time, as we constantly coin new words ("neologisms") and use existing words in new ways. A word gets its meaning in part from its position in a sentence. For example, we can recognize what happens when a noun becomes a verb: changing "party" from a noun to a verb doesn't alter the rules of grammar.

Any viable structure has to be self-regulating; everything in it has to follow the rules for combining elements. If my plastic dinosaur doesn't have a part that fits into a Tinkertoy wheel hole, it can't be part of my structure.

Language is self-regulating. If you add a new element,

Ferdinand de Saussure

it has to function as a part of speech, like a noun, verb, or adverb. If you add a new sound to speech, it doesn't necessarily become part of the structure of language unless it fits the rules of grammar. If you add a new graphic element to writing, it doesn't become part of the structure of language unless it can be recognized as meaningful.

OK, let's turn now to a specific structuralist analysis of language, as articulated by the Swiss linguist Ferdinand de Saussure in his classic text, *Course in General Linguistics* (1916).

Saussure asks a very basic question about language: How do words get their meaning? Common sense tells us that language is a NAMING process, through which objects and ideas get associated with a particular word. What I'm sitting on right now is called a "chair."

Though Saussure says this is a naïve view of how language works, it's also a useful one. It gets across the idea that a word always has two dimensions. A word is a *sound* that points to a *thing;* Saussure calls these two parts the "sound image" and the "concept."

A sound image is not just the physical sound you make with your mouth; it's also the psychological imprint of that sound, the impression it makes. (Think of talking to yourself—you don't necessarily make a sound, but you know what you are saying.) The concept is the object or idea that the sound image makes you think of.

A linguistic SIGN is made by the union of a sound image and a concept. Saussure says that the two parts of the sign are identifiable but inseparable, like two sides of a piece of paper. Hearing the sound image "tree" will always conjure a large plant with roots, branches, and leaves.

Saussure also calls the sound image the SIGNIFIER and the concept the SIGNIFIED. Together, a signifier and a signified create a sign.

Go over that last paragraph again, because this is a central idea in the literary theories we'll be talking about through the rest of this book.

So how does a signifier get connected to a signified? How does a word get connected to a thing?

Saussure's most important contribution to literary theory is the idea that...

The connection between signifier and signified is ARBITRARY.

There is no reason why a particular word means a particular thing, no reason why a specific sound image gets associated with a specific concept. Nothing in either

the word or the thing can explain how the two go together. There is no natural, intrinsic, logical, or spiritual relation between a sound image and a concept.

The most obvious evidence of this is that different languages have different words for the same thing. "Dog" is *dog* in English, *perro* in Spanish, *chien* in French, *hund* in German. If there were some inherent connection between word and object, you would expect that all languages would use the same signifier to represent the signified canine.

The idea of an ARBITRARY link between signifier and signified is one of the most important principles in literary theory. That characteristic makes it possible to separate the signifier and signified, and to change the relation between them. This means that a single signified can have multiple signifiers, and a single signifier can have multiple signifieds.

Imagine language as a spectrum. At one end is the dictionary definition: one word means one thing, one signifier is connected to one and only one signified, and meaning doesn't require interpretation or thought; meaning is unitary and totally transparent. At the opposite end is absolute fluidity of meaning, whereby one signifier can be connected to any signified, and whatever meaning you get from words comes entirely from your own interpretation.

Think of it this way: At the denotative end of the spectrum is a plumbing manual. You read it for its information; if it says "unscrew the pipe" you unscrew the pipe. At the opposite, connotative end of the spectrum is a work of literature—a poem. You read the poem to figure out its meaning; if it says "unscrew the pipe," you start wondering what signifieds might be connected to the signifiers "unscrew" and "pipe."

Mostly, we hang out somewhere close to the plumbing manual end of the spectrum, if only because we want to use words to communicate relatively clearly. If we had to interpret (or "close read") everything anyone said to us, we'd never get anything done!

On the other hand, literature—poetry in particular— loves to slip toward the more fluid end of the spectrum, to slide words away from a definitive single meaning and toward a multiplicity of meaning, ambiguity, and instability. That slipperiness is possible because the bond between signifier and signified is arbitrary.

But are the associations between signifier and signified *really* arbitrary? Aren't there any signs that are truly natural?

Saussure looks at signs that seem less arbitrary than others, ones that seem to have some kind of logical connection between signifier and signified. What about onomatopoeic words—those that sound like what they mean, like "pop" or "buzz"? Saussure argues that they are just as arbitrary as any signifier/signified combination because they are agreed-upon approximations in writing of certain sounds.

Another example: Animals say different things in different languages, because different languages transcribe their approximation of an animal's sound differently. A rooster in English says *cock-a-doodle-do,* while in Spanish it says *cocorico.*

Saussure is not at all interested in *how* communities agree on associating a particular signifier with a particular signified, nor on how signs change. Like all structuralists, he focuses on a SYNCHRONIC analysis of language as a system or structure. In other words, he examines it only in the present moment, without regard to its history or its future possibilities. Analyses that do take time into account, that look at the history of changes in a particular structure, are called DIACHRONIC.

So a sign is made of a signifier and a signified whose connection is arbitrary. Put a bunch of signs together and you have a SIGNIFYING SYSTEM. Remember making secret codes as a kid? You were making signifying systems. Any language, like English or French or Chinese, is a signifying system.

One of the main characteristics of any signifying system is LINEARITY. The signs in a signifying system operate in a linear sequence.

This is pretty obvious, but it's important. You can't say two words at the same time and have them both be intelligible. Signs are articulated in time, one word after the other. The same is true for written signs. You can't write two words in the same space and have both be legible. Written

signs require space between each sign; spoken words require time. Both speech and writing are linear.

The linearity of a sentence also comes from the rules of grammar that any language maintains. Different languages have different standard word orders—in French the adjective typically follows the noun, while in English the noun usually follows the adjective—but all languages have some way of controlling what order words come in. (Latin is an exception; words in Latin can be written in any order because the form of the word contains its own grammatical significance—a noun takes a different form than a verb).

The structure of English can be summed up in a single sentence:

The adjectival noun verbed the direct object adverbially into the prepositional phrase.

When you do connect a signifier and a signified, you make a linguistic sign. The meaning that sign creates is what Saussure calls **signification.** Signification is a positive relationship involving one sign in a signifying system; signification contrasts with what Saussure calls value.

Value is a complicated idea, if only because the word itself has a lot of other meanings in standard English—synonyms include worth, importance, usefulness, or desirability. For Saussure, a linguistic sign has value because it is not any other sign within a signifying system. Value is thus a negative relationship, a relationship of difference. In order

to determine value, you have to know all the elements of a signifying system and be able to see that any one element is different from any of the others.

The most basic example is binary computer code, which consists only of 1s and 0s: 1101010101010001001001010 is a signifying system for a computer, where the value of 1 is that it is not 0, and the value of 0 is that it is not 1.

As Saussure says, "Language is a system of interdependent terms in which the value of each term results solely from the simultaneous presence of the others."

To establish value, you have to look at a signifying system as a whole and see all the elements within it. This perspective is what Saussure calls *langue*, the French word for "language." Looking at a system on the level of langue enables you to see all the parts at once, and to notice that each sign is different from each other sign. By contrast, when you look at an individual sign, you are examining it at the level of *parole*, the French word for "word." When you examine a particular parole, you see the positive relation of signification; when you look at langue, you see the negative relations of value among all the elements.

Saussure says that meaning, within a signifying system, is always based on the RELATIONS that can occur between the units in the system. When we look at the level of parole—or individual signs—we see the arbitrary relationship between signifier and signified; when we look at the level of langue—or all the signs within a system—we see relations of difference, called **value**.

The linear relations of signs, constituting the grammar of a signifying system, create what Saussure calls "syntagmatic relations." These are phrases that make grammatical or syntactical sense, or meaning, even when they are taken out of the context of a full sentence. Our game of Mad Libs worked because all adjectives have the same syntagmatic relation to all nouns, all adverbs to all verbs, etc.

A signifying system can make meaning yet another way, particular to individual users of the system. Associative relations are meanings that come from things an individual language user associates with particular words or phrases. The phrase "you're out," for example, may have different meanings for someone who is a baseball fan than for someone who is gay.

Syntagmatic relations are important because they allow for new words—neologisms—to arise and be accepted into a linguistic community. "To google," for instance, has meaning because the noun "google" was moved to the position of verb, taking on a new syntagmatic position and relation to other words. Associative relations are important because they break patterns established in strictly grammatical/linear (syntagmatic) relations and allow for metaphoric expressions. "Literary" language, on the fluid end of the language spectrum, relies on associative relations (in addition to signification and value) to make meaning. Literal language, by contrast, relies on syntagmatic relations (in addition to signification and value) to make meaning.

Structural Anthropology and Claude Lévi-Strauss

Saussure shows us that a signifying system consists of units, or signs, that are put together according to rules, or grammar. He insists that the structure of any signifying system is linear: we determine the meaning of each unit, each sign, by reading one at a time. In English, we read from left to right; in Hebrew, we read from right to left; in Chinese, we read from top to bottom.

When you look at a signifying system on the level of the individual sign, or parole, you look at the (arbitrary) connection between signifier and signified. When you look at a signifying system as langue, you are looking at the system as a whole, including all the elements or signs within it. Value is the meaning produced by the fact that each sign within the system is different from each of the other signs.

Let's take the alphabet as an example. At the level of parole, "A" as signifier is connected to its signified, which is the sound we make when we say the letter out loud. At the level of langue, "A" is "A" because it is not B or C or D or Z. When you say what A is, as a sign, you are looking at the **presence** of A; when you look at what A is **not,** you are looking at the **absence** of all the other signs in the system. Thus, value is knowing the meaning of a sign by knowing the absence of all other possible signs.

Signifying systems are everywhere in our culture. The French structuralist critic and theorist Roland Barthes, in *Mythologies* (1957), argued that almost anything can become a sign when a signifier is connected to a signified. Think about cars as a signifying system: the car you drive says something about who you are. If you drive a BMW, you are assumed to be rich; if you drive a Prius, you are assumed to be environmentally oriented. And within the signifying system of cars, the Prius has value because it's not the BMW, or the Ford pickup truck, or the SUV, or the minivan. Barthes says that there are an almost infinite number of signifying systems in contemporary culture, if only because consumer choices become signifiers so easily.

This is one of the ways that structural analysis can be useful for the humanities, since part of our job is to read and interpret the ways cultures have of making meaning. Structuralism has been important in a variety of disciplines, such as linguistics, as we have seen. Claude Lévi-Strauss, another 20th-century Frenchman, adopted structuralism

Lévi-Strauss

as a methodology for anthropology because it allowed him to look for what is common among the vast variety of human cultures—what is universally true about the human condition.

Lévi-Strauss argues that every human culture that has ever existed has had underlying structures that organize aspects of existence. Among these are a signifying system, or linguistic structure; a mode of distribution and exchange of goods, called an economic structure; and a way to determine how relationships occur and what they mean, or a **kinship system.** Within a kinship system, the "units" are individual men and women; the rules for combining the units tell any specific culture who can marry whom and who is related to whom.

In *The Elementary Structures of Kinship* (1949), Lévi-Strauss points out that relationships form a primary organizing structure that depends on value—the relations among all of the elements in the system. For example, I am "daughter" in relation to my parents, "mother" in relation to my children, "niece" in relation to my mother's brother, and "aunt" in relation to my sister's children. I am always "me," but I have various names in different relationships. The possible relationships available within any particular society are what form the kinship system or structure. That structure generates meaning by naming a relationship ("niece" and "aunt"), which depends upon knowing all the other possible relationships within the structure.

Kinship systems create meanings for cultures by determining who can marry and reproduce with whom. The practice of exogamy—marrying someone outside your family or clan—is enforced via the recognition of kinship relations. In some cultures, it's OK to marry your first cousin, while in others it's not. Other relationships are also determined by position within a kinship system: for example, your position within the kinship system determines who you pay respect to, who you compete with, who you give gifts to, and who you receive gifts from; it often determines how goods get exchanged and who has power over whom.

The most important and constant structure that

organizes human cultures, according to Lévi-Strauss, is the **binary pair** or **binary opposition.** Think about it—in my class, we made a list, which could have gone on forever, of all the concepts that have this binary structure. Lévi-Strauss, in a book entitled *The Raw and the Cooked* (1964), insists that the binary opposition is the fundamental structure organizing ALL human cultures; it is universal.

We can (and will) argue with Lévi-Strauss about this. Certainly it is true for all Western cultures, since we can trace the idea of the binary opposition back to the Greeks—but whether it is true also for non-Western cultures should remain an open question.

Within every binary pair, Lévi-Strauss argues, one term is always favored over the other:

> Male/female
> Light/dark
> Good/evil
> Hot/cold
> Day/night
> Reason/madness
> Human/animal

The list can go on forever. But it's important to note that the things on the left side of the slash are often associated with each other, as do the things on the right side of the slash— "male" is associated with light, good, hot, day, reason, and human, while "female" is associated with dark, evil, cold, night, madness, and animal. Thus, you can "read" sets of binary oppositions in two ways: you can pair one thing with its opposite, or you can pair something on the left side of the slash with other things on the left side.

Now let's have a look at "The Structural Study of Myth," a 1955 essay by Lévi-Strauss that gives us another structuralist method for thinking about the ways literature makes meaning.

In myth, says Lévi-Strauss, ***anything can happen***. Myth is not limited by what is true, or even what is probable. Rather, in myth, "everything becomes possible." Gods can turn into animals, humans can turn into trees, things like that.

Nevertheless, Lévi-Strauss insists, myths are strikingly similar across cultures and time periods. So why is it that myths—stories that could say anything—often seem to tell the same story, regardless of cultural and historical differences?

His answer is that myths share a common **structure** that is a human universal.

Myth *is* language, Lévi-Strauss asserts; it is a signifying

system that operates just as any language does. He follows Saussure's idea that, at the level of langue, all signifying systems are alike in that all are made of units governed by rules, while at the level of parole, each signifying system is unique. Lévi-Strauss talks about the langue of myth as **reversible time**, corresponding to Saussure's idea of the synchronic aspect of langue. Reversible time is when you step into the time machine and the structure you're looking at remains the same, regardless of whether you go back in time or forward in time. At the level of parole, he says, **non-reversible time** is in operation: the same signifier could be connected to a different signified in the past and will be connected to a different signified in the future.

Lévi-Strauss cites the French Revolution as an example of a myth that demonstrates both reversible and non-reversible time. I'll use the American Revolution to make the same points.

The American Revolution is an event that happened in

the past; it has a definite end point, and it is not still going on. Thus, it is an example of non-reversible time. We often invoke the American Revolution, especially in politics, as an event that has a timeless set of values that are still very much in action in the United States. If you ever watch a presidential debate, notice how often the candidates evoke "the Founding Fathers" and their ideals. This is an example of reversible time. We can pull up "the American Revolution" at any time, past or future, as if it always has the same meaning.

Remember the binary pairs this way:

Historical	*Ahistorical*
Parole	*Langue*
Non-reversible	*Reversible*

In this sense, the American Revolution, like the French Revolution, is a **myth**. It happened, but it is invoked as if it is timeless.

Lévi-Strauss gives us another way of thinking about a myth by contrasting it with poetry. Myth/poetry is another binary opposition! Poetry, he argues, is that which cannot be paraphrased; a poem exists exactly and only in the words written by the poet, and you can't change those words without changing the poem itself. A myth, however, can always be "translated" or paraphrased—told a different way—and still remain itself. Unlike poetry, *myth is story*, and stories are malleable. They can take many different shapes and still retain the same basic elements in the same structural relations. Think again about stepmother-prince-princess as the elements. The structural relations between stepmother and princess, and between prince and princess, remain the same regardless of the names of the characters.

From a structuralist (or Formalist) perspective, all stories or narratives have certain basic elements which all versions of a story retain. A Russian Formalist named Vladimir Propp analyzed Russian folktales and found that all of them contained at least one of thirty-one basic structures; they differed only in the details of the story.

A structuralist analysis of narrative might do the same thing: find the overall structures of all story types, and then classify every example of a story by type. This would be a finite and ultimately boring project: take a story, put it in its proper pigeonhole, and that's it—done.

The real **meaning** in myth, according to Lévi-Strauss, lies not in the individual elements, but in the patterns that shape how the elements combine and form relations with each other.

He then discusses the basic unit of myth, which he names a **mytheme,** analogous to a phoneme, morpheme, or sememe in linguistics.

The true constituent units of a myth, says Lévi-Strauss, are not the isolated units or mythemes, but the "bundles of relations" that structure how those mythemes are combined.

The structure of a myth or story is thus two-dimensional, not linear. This is an important way that myth or story differs from language.

To illustrate these two dimensions, Lévi-Strauss imagines future space aliens finding the remnants of human culture on Earth (post-apocalypse) and trying to figure out what human culture was all about by looking at the remnants. If the aliens were in a library, they might be able to decipher written language if they could determine the correct direction for reading the line of print—left to right, right to left, top to bottom, etc. But they would be baffled if they found a musical score, which is read from left to right in time for the melody, but up and down, synchronically, for the harmony or chords.

And that's the structure of story or myth: it reads in two dimensions, like a music score. The narrative is read left to right, unfolding in time (first this happens, then this happens); the bundles of relations read in columns, like the harmony in music, are called "theme."

Lévi-Strauss gives an extremely long and detailed reading of the Oedipus myth. In my class, I use "Goldilocks and the Three Bears" as a much easier and more familiar example.

	Papa Bear	Mama Bear	Baby Bear
Porridge	*too hot*	*too cold*	*just right*
Chair	*too big*	*too small*	*just right*
Bed	*too hard*	*too soft*	*just right*

When we read this structure from left to right, we get the story. When we read it for the bundles of relations, we see that Papa Bear is hot, big, and hard, while Mama Bear is cold, small, and soft. You get the idea.

A myth always contains at least one set of cultural contradictions—expressed as binary opposites—and progresses from an awareness of those oppositions toward their resolution. Lévi-Strauss reads this as a kind of Hegelian dialectic: two opposing terms are mediated by a third term, which becomes one side of a new binary opposition.

In the Goldilocks story, the cultural contradiction might be a human breaking into a bear's house—or the contradiction that bears live in houses and eat porridge. When we lay out the story like a musical score, we can see also that "Baby Bear" resolves the binary oppositions between Papa Bear and Mama Bear, being "just right." Goldilocks occupies the position of Baby Bear—so is she also resolving the binary oppositions? In the end, however, she gets kicked out (in some versions, eaten), leaving the original structure in place. So what does the Goldilocks myth mean? What contradictions does it resolve?

At the end of "The Structural Study of Myth," Lévi-Strauss argues that myth is often seen as a "primitive" way of thinking about cultural relations, events, and contradictions, in opposition to a more "civilized" way of thinking, which we call **science**. But if myth has its own structure, it also has its own **logic**. Lévi-Strauss argues that myth is just as "ordered" and "logical" a mode of thinking as science. It's not that we humans have gotten smarter as we've developed from "primitive" to "civilized," it's just that our means of reasoning have changed, from myth or story to scientific methodology.

Note here that Lévi-Strauss accepts the modern Western cultural idea that science is the only form of "true" knowledge, arguing that myth is just as "scientific" as science and not necessarily an inferior way of knowing—just different. But that's a deconstructive idea, so let's move on to the next chapter.

Chapter 3

DECONSTRUCTION

I have two textbooks in front of me. The first is *Critical Theory Since Plato*; it was one of my textbooks in graduate school in the 1980s. The second is *Critical Theory Since 1965*; it has been one of the textbooks I use in my "Introduction to Literary Theory" course.

Think about the time spans: *Critical Theory Since Plato* covers more than 2,000 years of thinking and writing about literature, while the other volume—just as massive—covered a mere twenty-one years when it was first published in 1986. Clearly, something very important

happened around 1965 that changed the way that critical theory, or "literary theory," thought.

What happened was an academic conference, held at Johns Hopkins University in Baltimore, Maryland, that brought structuralist thinkers to the United States for the first time. Almost all the "big names" of structuralism were there: René Girard, Georges Poulet, Lucien Goldmann,

Jacques Derrida

Tzvetan Todorov, Roland Barthes, Jacques Lacan, and Jacques Derrida.

The conference, held in October 1966, was titled "The Languages of Criticism and the Sciences of Man." It was intended to open a dialogue between the French intellectuals who were redefining *les sciences humaines,* the human sciences, and their American academic counterparts, who were becoming increasingly dismayed by the humanist insistence that meaning and interpretation are anti-rational, therefore subjective, forms of knowing.

From Plato to the mid-1960s, literary theories had focused on the mimetic, didactic, expressive, affective, and formal dimensions of literature. With structuralism came an analysis of literature as impersonal; meaning comes not from the artist or the reader or their interaction, but from the mechanical operations of language itself. Structuralism promised to offer to literary studies a methodology with

the objectivity that had been lacking from previous modes of analysis. Structuralism would put literary modes of knowing on the same footing with scientific modes of knowing.

Scientific knowledge is rational, reproducible, and verifiable. The scientific method is a system of ongoing testing and continual verification of objective explanations of observable phenomena, which, for Western culture at least, always produces "truth." Thus, the goal of the human sciences, as represented at the Baltimore conference in 1966, was to examine and understand language, literature, culture, the soul, the mind, and the unconscious through a shared scientific methodology: structuralism.

The conference celebrating structuralism's introduction to American academics was disrupted, however, by Jacques Derrida's discussion of the uncertainty of language itself. Derrida laid open the question of whether language can ever say anything that is "true."

A Brief Excursion Through Western Metaphysics

To understand the importance of Derrida's revelation, we need first to take a quick tour through Western philosophy and the question of truth. So let's get in a time machine and move backward from the mid-1960s to the time of Plato (circa 350 BCE).

Plato talked about two kinds of knowledge: *episteme* and *techne. Techne* is the knowledge of how to do things—hence the word "technology." *Techne* as technical knowledge stands in contrast to *episteme,* which is how we think about things; epistemology is the study of how we know what we know. *Episteme* also stood in contrast to *doxa,* which were popular beliefs or opinions, like myths or religious beliefs, which rely on faith rather than on knowledge.

For Plato, *episteme* was superior to *techne.* With technical knowledge, all you can do is make stuff; with epistemic knowledge, you can investigate the idea of knowledge itself and look for what Plato called "justified true belief."

Literature, for Plato, was a kind of art or craft, a kind of *techne,* consisting largely of the arts of rhetoric, drama, and poetry.

The idea of "justified true belief" is the foundation for most, if not all, of Western philosophy. The central question is, "How do we know what we know?" And, more importantly, "How do we know that what we know is TRUE?"

This is a question that haunts Western philosophy. How can we find what Immanuel Kant called *a priori* knowledge—something that is true no matter what? We need to find something that will function the way an axiom functions in geometry, as a starting point, a solid unshakeable foundation on which to build our ideas about the world, our worldviews, our ways of thinking, our epistemologies.

For Plato, the guarantee of Truth was the Forms—perfect, eternal, unchanging—which are the template for everything that exists in the imperfect material world. The everyday world we live in is merely a copy of something much better, but the existence of Forms guarantees that even our flawed copies have an ultimate stable referent.

Another way to think about Plato's Forms is that they are Transcendental Signifieds. If everything in the material world is a signifier, what they point to (their signifieds) are the Forms that preceded it. I know what my water bottle is because it's a copy of an ideal version that exists without material substance.

Note that, for Plato, words were forms of representation of things and ideas—a word had meaning because it stood in for the thing, which was itself a copy of an ideal Form. Words were thus two removes away from the ultimate reality of Forms.

The history of Western philosophy might be read as the history of this search for stable Transcendental Signifieds, for some answer to the question "How do we know that what we know is true?"

The rise of the Judeo-Christian belief systems brought a new answer to that question: God.

God creates the world and guarantees that that world is real. God becomes, in this sense, the ultimate guarantor of the truth of our knowledge.

Let's look at that more closely, because the Judeo-Christian account of the creation of the world in Genesis lays out some very important patterns in Western epistemology.

God says, "Let there be light," and there is light. And light is separated from darkness. God creates the first binary opposition, and He saw that it was good.

Creation in Genesis proceeds to God making all the basic binary oppositions: day/night, land/sea, sky/earth, human/animal, male/female. These binary pairs become part of the pattern for the ways Judeo-Christian culture thinks about the world and itself: the binary opposition is the structure of our knowledge.

Jacques Derrida, in the 20th century, focused on two

binaries that he says are particularly important in the history of Western philosophy: speech/writing and presence/absence. In Western philosophy, speech is generally regarded as more important than writing. This may not be as evident as the example of light/dark, but it's true in terms of linguistic theories. Speech is posited as a first or primary form of language, while writing is understood merely as the transcription of speech. Speech gets privileged over writing because speech is aligned with presence: for  there to be spoken language, somebody (in the age before sound recording) had to be there to do the speaking.

This idea of the person, the self, who does the speaking is part of the metaphysics of presence. The idea of presence is central to most systems of Western philosophy from Plato until 1966. Presence is the positive side of the binary opposition presence/absence. Speech is associated with presence, and both are favored over writing and absence; this privileging of speech and presence is called **logocentrism**.

The idea that speech = presence in Genesis guarantees that God exists because God speaks. God's presence is the guarantee of truth. The structure of truth, created by God, is binary oppositions.

Let's move on to the 17th century. Philosophy is beginning to move away from God as the sole transcendental signified, the source of knowledge and truth. Instead, it begins looking to the concept of "the self"—the mind, the soul, the human individual, the present thing doing  the speaking—as the origin of knowledge and truth.

The French philosopher René Descartes, in 1637, wrestles with the question, "What do I know for sure, without any doubt, on my own, without reference to anything outside of me?" Descartes argued that consciousness can't be based solely on sensory perception, because the body can make mistakes in processing the external world—sensory perceptions can be deceptive. So he imagines all kinds of possibilities for doubt, including the idea that his perceptions of the external world are a dream, perhaps even an illusion produced by demons to torment him.

René Descartes

All I can know with absolute certainty, says Descartes, is that I think. I perceive myself as thinking about this question of what I can know for sure. Maybe I can't know any-

thing else except the fact that I think. Hence his proclamation...

"I think, therefore I am"—the Cartesian *cogito ergo sum*.

The Cartesian notion of the thinking self as the transcendental signified helped emphasize other binary oppositions, including mind/body and self/other. Let's take a look at them for a moment.

The mind/body binary is pretty familiar—we know that our bodies "betray" us with faulty, false, or incomplete information. We can only try to locate truth in the mind; we see the body as inferior and perhaps threatening to the mind's powers of logic and rationality. Descartes gives a name to the knowing self—he calls it "I". The "I" is the thing that does the thinking; "I" designates the concept of selfhood, of "I"dentity. (Descartes posits the "I" as an a priori entity. It preexists the act of thinking. Consciousness creates itself.)

"I" also holds a structural position in English grammar—the position of the subject of a sentence. But "I", like most pronouns, is a notoriously unstable signifier.

Roman Jakobson, a Russian American linguist, pointed out that pronouns are "shifters"—they are signifiers that shift meaning depending on who says them. They are the "tricksters" of linguistic structure. So when I say "I", I mean

something different than when you say "I". Each of us refers to this thing we call a self, my uniqueness, my "I"dentity as different and separate from everyone else—my self is not your self. But we both use the signifier "I" to refer to two different selves.

So "I", like most pronouns, is not a stable signifier; it does not point to a single signified. But Descartes (writing more than three centuries before Jakobson) didn't recognize this. He discovered a fundamental truth on which he could build a reliable mode of knowing: *cogito ergo sum* places the human power of thought at the top of the hierarchy of ways of knowing.

In Western thought, the "I" that thinks is "rational man." And by the 18th century, rational man has developed the scientific method to investigate the physical world and discover objective truth.

OK, let's return now to 1966 in Baltimore. Structuralism is being celebrated, welcomed to the United States as a refreshingly scientific way to think about the "human sciences," including literary studies. Structuralist linguistics have enabled us to understand the problem of the Cartesian "I"; Saussure has explained the arbitrariness of the connection between signifier and signified as a way to detach "I" as a grammatical structure, a pronoun, from the concept of "the self" as the transcendental signified.

Which means that all of us who study ourselves—those dedicated to the "human sciences," including literary studies—have some objective methodology on which to base our perceptions and arguments. Finally we can be just like scientists and produce truth.

Until Jacques Derrida delivered his conference paper, "Structure, Sign, and Play in the Discourse of the Human Sciences" and informed the eminent transatlantic structuralist community that truth is impossible because language can have no stable meaning.

Structures, Signs, and Centers

"Things fall apart; the center cannot hold."—W. B. Yeats

Unlike Saussure, who looked at the structure of language as linear, and Lévi-Strauss, who looked at the two-dimensional structure of story, Derrida insists that all structures need some sort of center that holds them together. He's talking about the 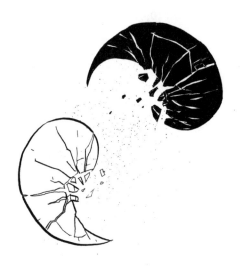 history of Western metaphysics as we've just reviewed it. All philosophical systems, or worldviews, posit something that is their origin, their god-term, which is the a priori foundation of their epistemic viewpoint.

According to Derrida, the **center** is the crucial part of any structure. It's the point where you can't substitute anything. In the rest of the structure, you can substitute one element for another, move things around, as long as you follow the rules. But there can be only one center, and no other element can take its place.

Derrida insists that the center of any system is a peculiar part. It is the thing that created the system in the first place, but it isn't governed by the rules of the system. The center of a system has no equivalent value; nothing can replace it or be exchanged for it. It is the cause and ultimate referent—the transcendental signified—for everything in the system.

The center, for Derrida, is thus a weird part of a system or structure—it's part of the structure, but not part of it, because it is the governing element. As he puts it, the center is the part of the structure that "escapes structurality."

Thus, paradoxically, the center is both within the structure and outside it. The center is the center, but it is not part of what Derrida calls "the totality"; so the center is *not* the center. The concept of the centered structure, according to Derrida, is "contradictorily coherent."

IT'S OK IF YOUR BRAIN IS STARTING TO HURT NOW!

One example of a centered system from the tradition of Western metaphysics is the Judeo-Christian belief system. God is the center; God creates the world but doesn't have to follow the rules (the rules of nature, for example; God can do "miracles"). God holds all the elements of His system in place and ensures that everything has stable meaning.

Another example, perhaps less abstract, is a classroom. Imagine yourself in an auditorium or lecture hall with seats bolted to the floor. You come in and occupy a seat; perhaps you sit in the same seat for each class session. The seat is your subject position; it's the point from which you see the world around you.

Then I come in. I am the Professor, and I occupy my position behind the lectern. When I start to speak, you are quiet (perhaps even taking notes). Then for fifty minutes, I talk and you listen—you don't move around, you don't leave, you don't talk or surf (as far as I know). I get to talk, and you get to do whatever it is you do.

You are subject to my rules and regulations; I am the center of the system that is the class and you are an inhabitant of the structure I've created. I make the assignments for the class but don't have to do them; I don't have to follow my own rules. This works whether you are in my class, where you are Student and I am Professor, or whether you are reading this book, where you are Reader and I am Author. Either way, you do what I say!

A center stabilizes a structure and fixes or stops motion, which Derrida calls "play." If the Professor is there, the students stay in their seats; if the Professor doesn't show up, the students can "play" or move as they like.

A center provides what Derrida calls "full

presence," which takes us back to the presence/absence binary discussed earlier. Full presence is where there is no absence—where the slash between the two terms holds firm and where "presence" has the absolutely stable meaning of "not absence."

Language, says Derrida, has no center. There is no "god-term" or center that holds a signifier in place with a signified to create stable meaning. The structure of language that Saussure described, where the connection between a signifier and a signified is arbitrary, means that any signifier can be connected to—or disconnected from—any signified.

We use language as if there were definite and precise meanings to each word, using tools like a dictionary to provide authoritative meaning. But when you look up a word in a dictionary, what do you get? More words, which you then look up in the dictionary...

"Il n'ya pas hors de texte," says Derrida. There is nothing outside of the text, no actual referent or object that a word represents. There is only language, only signifiers, whose meaning depends upon other signifiers.

Because the connection between signifier and signified is slippery, loosey-goosey, and "poetic," meaning is always sliding away—it can never be fixed, stable, definite, or reliable.

Think of it this way: every signifier has positive meaning (Saussure's "signification") when connected to a single signified.

"Chair" = the thing you sit on

But every signifier also has value, according to Saussure, which means that each signifier is different from every other signifier. Every signifier therefore carries with it the "ghost" or trace of all the words it isn't; every signifier contains the absence of all other possible words.

Chair is not hair is not hail is not hale is not kale is not male is not made is not maid....

This, in a nutshell, is what Derrida calls **_différance_**. The term comes from the French verb _différer,_ which means both "to differ" and "to defer." Note the spelling. In French, _différance_ sounds exactly the same as _difference,_ but the distinction appears when you write the word. Derrida does this to highlight and to reverse the hierarchy of speech/writing.

The meaning of a signifier comes from its difference from every other signifier in the system; the meaning of a one signifier has to be deferred to the next signifier, and the next, and the next, and so on. You can never come to definitive meaning because you always have to look to the next signifier in the never-ending chain of language. You can never get to fixed, stable, unitary, or fully present meaning. You can't say what any word means with any degree of certainty. ***There can be no "truth" in language!***

The interpreters of texts, codes, and other signifying systems are left with trying to articulate what Edward Said called "the vacant spaces between things, ideas, and words."

We can, and do, try to make language behave, settle down, and have stable meaning, but we have to install some kind of center in order to do that. Dictionaries, teachers, and mothers often serve as centers to enforce correct language. For example, a professor (in a university English department especially!) has the authority to tell you, when you write a

paper or essay, that your grammar is right or wrong; she has the power to "punish" you for using incorrect grammar by giving you a lower grade on the assignment.

I have a sign in my office: "I am silently correcting your grammar." It strikes terror into everyone's heart.

OK, back to Derrida. In "Structure, Sign, and Play in the Discourse of the Human Sciences," his paper delivered at the Baltimore conference, Derrida analyzes Lévi-Strauss's idea that cultural structures are built on binary oppositions. He wants to know how stable or secure these structures really are.

The logic of the binary opposition appears in the formula A = not B. Everything that belongs to category A has to be different from everything that belongs to category B; there can be no overlaps, no element that belongs to both sides of a binary opposition.

Lévi-Strauss had seen the basic structures of all cultural organizations as binary opposites, where one term had meaning or value because it was not the other term. The dichotomy "culture/nature," he argued, is the model or core for any and all structures of a particular culture. Lévi-Strauss defined "nature" as that which is universal, or common to all cultures. He defines "culture" as that which is specific to each individual human organization; culture is to nature as specific is to universal.

It is here that Derrida discovers in Lévi-Strauss what he calls "a scandal." *Mon dieu!* There is an element of social organization that belongs to both sides of the fundamental binary. And that element is incest—not the act itself, but the idea of incest as breaking the boundaries or rules of a social order.

The idea of incest is universal—every culture has rules about what constitutes "family" and what relationships can and cannot be (reproductively) sexual. But each culture makes its own rules about incest. In some cultures, it's OK to marry your first cousin; in other cultures it's not OK. The scandal for Derrida is that incest belongs both to culture and to nature, both universal and specific.

And that is deconstruction in a nutshell. You find a logic or premise that depends on a binary opposition, and then you look for where that binary pair becomes shaky or starts to fall apart.

Here's another example: hot/cold. There is no specific temperature at which something is definitively "hot" or "cold"—the terms have meaning only in contrast to each other. What is hot is not cold; what is cold is not hot.

Note that deconstruction is NOT the process of finding a middle point between two binary opposites. "Warm" is not the deconstruction of "hot/cold."

Another example might be "male/female" (a binary we'll be talking about a lot in upcoming chapters!). A transgendered person deconstructs the male/female binary.

All right, fine. So Derrida read his paper at the 1966 conference and said that we can't ever know for sure what words mean; we can't rely on language to have stable meaning. So what? Does the world fall apart? Does my butt slide off the thing I sit on because there can't be a definitive meaning for "chair"?

No, of course not. But what does fall apart is a worldview, an episteme. If "truth" is what we can know for

certain—for sure, absolutely and always—then truth is impossible because absolute meaning in language is impossible. If we can't think without words, if there is no way to talk about language objectively from outside it, then there can be no full presence, no absolute certainty ... or science.

Science itself depends upon the idea of objectivity, of being outside the thing you are investigating. But when the object of investigation has anything to do with language, you can't be outside it. What we've been searching for in Western metaphysics since Plato can't exist, isn't possible. Moreover, science depends upon being able to perform a particular speech act to "state facts." But if language is fundamentally unstable, can anything you state be "factual?"

So now what? Once you deconstruct a system by pointing out its inconsistencies, once you show where there is play in a structure or where the center cannot hold,

Derrida says you have two choices. One is to throw out the whole structure and try to build another one without inconsistencies, contradictions, or play. But of course, according to Derrida, that's impossible. Building a new structure merely substitutes one center for another; the new center, or transcendental signified, again creates the mere illusion of fixed and stable "truth."

The other option is to keep using the original structure but to recognize that it is flawed. For Derrida, this means to stop attributing "truth value" to a structure or system and, instead, to reveal how "truth" is produced by a central idea that holds the whole system together. When you remove that center, the system falls apart, and you can "play" with its elements.

Derrida (and Lévi-Strauss) call this method **bricolage**, and the person who does it a *bricoleur*. A bricoleur is someone who doesn't care about the purity or stability or "truth" of a system; rather, she takes pieces of a flawed system and uses them to do what she wants.

Psychoanalysis, which we'll explore in the next chapter, offers a useful example. I can use words like "unconscious" and "Oedipus complex" in useful, meaningful ways even though I think the system or theory these terms refer to is seriously flawed.

My kids' playroom provides another good illustration. My kids have a lot of toys: a complete set of Legos, of Play-Doh, of alphabet blocks, and of countless other sets with thousands of tiny pieces. Each set was complete when they

unwrapped the package on Christmas or a birthday; two days later, the elements of the set had joined the chaos of all the others. Legos were stacked up with alphabet blocks, Barbie was covered in Play-Doh, and nothing was in its proper box. This is bricolage. My kids don't care that you're supposed to play with toy sets according to any rules, they just play with whatever is at hand, not caring about purity or coherence or equivalences. They make use of whatever is at hand to do whatever it is that catches their attention at the moment.

Derrida contrasts the bricoleur with the engineer. The engineer designs things, like buildings, which have to be stable and have little or no play, no movement. The engineer is the guy who thinks he is the center of his own discourse, the origin of his own language. The engineer is an "I" who knows that his rational mind, using the scientific method, will discover/create truth.

I am an engineer when I try to clean up the playroom and put all the toy pieces back in their proper boxes and systems!

The idea of bricolage provides a new way to talk and think about systems without falling into the trap of building a new system, with a new and improved center, out of the ruins of an old one. It offers a way to think about signifying systems without a transcendental signified.

Poststructuralism

So, after all that, what is deconstruction?

A) To define it is to limit it, to affirm that a single signifier can be firmly attached to a single signified, thus validating the logocentric structure of Western metaphysics.

B) A method of reading the text against itself.

C) Writing about writing about writing about writing about writing about writing...

D) Sheer and utter nonsense.

E) All of the above.

Deconstruction is what shook up the scientific certainty of structuralism.

After the Baltimore conference in 1966, a new episteme—a new worldview or mode of thinking—emerged: **poststructuralism**. Poststructuralism was a shift in the tectonic plates of Western cultural thought, a shift in how we theorize. Poststructuralism made the world linguistic in the same way that physicists after Einstein made the world mathematical.

Poststructuralism acknowledges that, when you write or speak, you can't mean exactly what you say. That's why so many poststructuralist theorists write incomprehensibly: to write clearly would be to assume that language can operate with the certainty and authority we thought it had in the humanist tradition and that we attribute to scientific discourses. If you try to define or categorize ideas, you attempt to present them as if they were absolute, fixed, definitive, and total, rather than unstable and provisional. So poststructuralists sometimes write as if the purpose of language is to obscure definitive meaning rather than to present and clarify an argument.

When we get to Jacques Lacan (in the next chapter), we'll see that "to understand" something, like deconstruction, always has to be said or written in quotes, because we have to acknowledge that there really is no such thing as "understanding." To understand, for Lacan, is to misunderstand; to think you grasp a stable truth or idea or word is to misunderstand the instability of language, thought, and reality.

So what do we do? We pretend that language has stable meaning, and we refer to that pretense through **irony**—the rhetorical ability to say two contradictory things at once.

The poststructuralist worldview presents the following ideas:

1. Things we have thought of as constant, including the notion of our own "I"dentity, are not stable and fixed, but fluid, changing, and unstable. Rather than being innate essences, the qualities of "I"dentity are socially constructed. Many of the theories examined in the chapters that follow are concerned with how such identities—such as gender, race, sexuality, and class—are constructed so that they feel as though they are constant and "true" and "natural."

2. Everything one thinks or does is in some degree the product of one's past experiences, one's beliefs, one's ideologies: there is no such thing as objectivity. Whereas

formalists, structuralists, and scientists claim that they can look at an object without any preconceived notions of what they will find, they are only masking their own ideological positioning.

3. Language is the most important factor in shaping our thinking about everything. Rather than reflecting the real world, language creates and structures everything we can know or think about "reality." We do not speak language, language speaks us; we are the inhabitants or products of the structure of language itself.

4. Because all "truth" is relative, all supposedly "essential" constants are fluid; language determines reality, but there is no such thing as definitive meaning. There is only and always ambiguity, fluidity, and multiplicity of meaning.

5. Everything that signifies is "text" and can be interpreted. Interpretation has no endpoint, consummation, or "truth." There is nothing outside of the text.

6. Because of the relativity of truth, there can be no such thing as a "total" theory, one that explains every aspect of some event or field.

Keep these premises in mind as we move forward into the world of poststructuralist literary theory.

Chapter 4
PSYCHOANALYSIS

All right, you need to know this now. I'm a feminist, and a lot of Freud's writings make me laugh out loud—or yell. His views of women are sexist and absurd.

And yet he is one of the most important thinkers of the 20th century: His system of psychoanalysis spawned countless versions of psychotherapy, and provided a new worldview or framework through which to comprehend the human mind's unconscious creation of literature, art, religion, sex, and the family.

Sigmund Freud

He began his career as a medical doctor in Vienna in the last decades of the 19th century. He treated patients for "hysteria"—a kind of catch-all term for symptoms that could not be traced to physiological causes. Most hysterics were women.

Sigmund Freud

Puzzling over the connections between mind and body, Freud argued that hysterics suffered from a mental disorder rather than a physical one. He then worked out a method to "read" what the hysteric's body was acting out and to use *talking* as a means of cure.

The idea of "talk therapy" begins with Freud. What was affecting hysterics, he determined, was a past trauma of some kind that they had repressed or forgotten. To cure them, Freud got them to talk about their lives.

Of course, anything so traumatic as to cause hysterical symptoms couldn't be remembered consciously. So Freud decided that the repressed memories of traumatic events reside in the mind in *the unconscious;* his therapeutic method entailed exploring the unconscious with his patients in order to unearth the traumatic memory and thereby banish it.

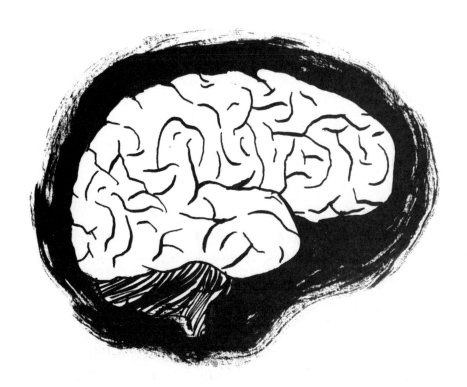

Freud's model of the mind posited a firm boundary between consciousness and the unconscious; a person uses psychic energy to keep repressed thoughts and memories from becoming conscious. Freud saw the cause of neurosis—which, he suggested, is endemic to Western civilization—as the need for excessive amounts of energy to maintain the force of repressing forbidden sexual feelings.

In *The Interpretation of Dreams* (1900), Freud praised dreams as "the royal road to the unconscious"—the fast lane to what was going on in that part of the mind that the conscious self can't know. Dreams use metonymic and metaphoric tropes, just as literary texts do.

> *Metaphor* and *metonymy* are rhetorical means of associating two unlike things by substituting one for the other.
>
> **Metaphor** is an equation between two disparate things—"Love is a rose."
>
> **Metonymy** is a way of identifying something by referring to an object associated with it—referring to "the crown" instead of the king or queen.

Dreams thus became, in psychoanalytic theory, a form of text that could be read and interpreted. Psychoanalysis has always been particularly attractive to literary critics, as it offers endless opportunities for hermeneutic interpretation: ways of looking for the "deeper meaning" or "real meaning."

For Freud, meaning resides in the unconscious. In addition to dreams, he points to jokes as a road into the unconscious as well as *parapraxes*—what are called "Freudian slips." Mistakes in speaking (or typing!) are not accidents, according to Freud; rather, they reveal some repressed idea that has slipped out through the barrier between the unconscious and conscious minds. Almost

anything you say or do can thus become a text to be read within a psychoanalytic framework.

Freud's talking cure encouraged patients to talk without censoring themselves, to tell stories or narrate dreams, which would reveal clues about what was going on in the unconscious mind. Freud and the patient would work to decode these clues, to read the drama that was being enacted by the hysteric's body. By decoding the symbols within the patient's unconscious, Freud hoped that the original trauma causing the hysteria would surface and that

the patient could then work with the memory that had been repressed (forbidden to enter the conscious mind).

In working with hysteric patients, Freud began to believe that the original trauma was related to sex. Women patients told him stories of being sexually molested as children by an older male figure. Freud eventually decided that these women were telling the story of a FANTASY— secretly *wishing* to have sex with their fathers—rather than hearing their stories as truth. From that (mis)interpretation sprang the fundamental story of Freudian psychoanalysis: the Oedipus complex.

Ok, let's move on.

Psychoanalysis tells a story of human development, a story that Freud thought was universal. In his book *Civilization and its Discontents* (1930), he argued that humans are pleasure-seeking animals; we like to do what feels good. For Freud, ALL pleasurable feelings are SEXUAL feelings: all pleasure is sexual pleasure. The pursuit of sexual pleasure, he said, is innate and instinctual. What he called **libido** is the force that drives the unconscious mind, the **id.**

The unconscious mind tells us to pursue pleasure and avoid pain: that is "the pleasure principle." Its twin, and binary opposite, is "the reality principle." This is the force that tells us to forego the pursuit of pleasure directly and to sublimate sexual or libidinal energy into doing things like art, music, building civilizations, etc.

The id, or unconscious, is pushing for pleasure. Its counterpart, the **superego** or conscience, is pulling for sublimation and work. The self, or **ego**, is caught in between! How does the self choose, with one voice saying *"sex!"* and the other saying *"work!"*?

Luckily for us, our first experiences as infants involve pleasure—sucking is our first mode of attaining pleasure as

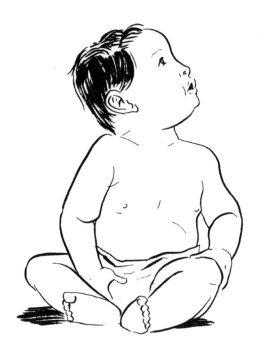

well as nourishment. (And remember, for Freud, all pleasure is sexual. So when we say the baby has sexual feelings, it doesn't necessarily mean genital orgasmic sexuality.) Freud labels this stage of development the **ORAL phase**, when the infant derives pleasure primarily through its mouth via sucking.

The baby does not yet have any awareness of itself as a separate being; it is not yet a "self" differentiated from other "selves." The baby doesn't know that its caregiver is a separate being—it's kind of a big blob. All it knows is the pleasurable feeling of sucking. During the oral phase, the infant starts to learn or construct unconscious distinctions between "inside" and "outside," which will be the basis for its sense of "self."

I refer to the infant as "it" because Freud says the infant does not yet have a gender identity: both male and female infants experience the same active, libidinal drives for pleasure. Freud then defines "masculine" as active and "feminine" as passive.

Until the drama of the Oedipus complex, the little girl is a little boy because both are actively seeking pleasure.

Until experiencing the Oedipus complex, the infant is *polymorphously perverse*, seeking anything and everything that is pleasurable. As all parents know, a baby's first move

will be to put an object in its mouth because it learned in the oral phase that putting things in your mouth feels good.

During the **ANAL phase** of development, the infant learns that pooping feels good and that having Mom clean you up after pooping also feels good. Freud associates the anal phase with learning to expel or push things out (another lesson in self boundaries) and with anger.

Finally, in the **PHALLIC phase**, the infant learns that touching its genitals feels good. And again, it feels especially good when Mom does it. And here is where the drama of OEDIPUS begins.

Oedipus, in Greek mythology, was the son of King Laius and Queen Jocasta of Thebes. An oracle predicted that Oedipus would kill his father and marry his mother. To keep that from happening, his parents wounded his feet and left him outside to die. But some shepherds found him and brought him to their city, Corinth, whose King Polybus and Queen Merope took him in and raised him.

As a young man, Oedipus hears about the prophecy and, believing Polybus and Merope to be his father and mother, leaves Corinth. On the road, he meets an older man and kills

him after a quarrel. Upon arriving in Thebes, Oedipus finds the city in mourning for its king and under the control of the Sphinx. Oedipus solves the Sphinx's riddle and thereby wins the crown and the hand of the widowed Queen Jocasta. Not until after they marry (and have four kids) does Oedipus find out that the man he killed was his father. Oedipus blinds himself in remorse.

The Oedipus myth as interpreted by Freud: The male child has a primary libidinal cathexis (erotic/sexual connection) with his mother's body; he first learns to associate (sexual) pleasure with Mom taking care of him as an infant. He is jealous of Dad, who "possesses" Mom and can take her away from him whenever he wants to. Dad is thus the source of Mom's absence, which for the boy means the absence of pleasurable feelings. The boy then hates Dad and wants to get rid of him. So he fantasizes about killing his father and "marrying" his mother.

This is the boy's Oedipus complex. Freud says it emerges between the ages of three and six. Sometime around that age, the boy makes a shocking discovery: he sees a girl naked for the first time, and he sees that SHE HAS NO PENIS!

The boy is horrified and terrified, says Freud. What happened to it? Did it get cut off? Was she being punished for something terrible? Could MY penis get cut off??

In short, the boy has *castration anxiety*. He values his penis above all other sources of pleasure. He is scared his might disappear like the girl's did.

And so enters into the **Castration Complex,** telling himself that Dad cut off the girl's penis because she was playing with it and thinking of Mom, and Dad got mad. The boy becomes afraid that Dad will cut off his penis because

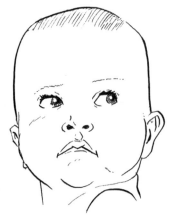

he touches it and thinks of Mom. He thinks that Dad will know about his murderous thoughts, too.

So the boy makes a deal: he promises to **REPRESS** his desire for Mom, creating a boundary between the unconscious and the conscious mind. He internalizes Dad's angry, punishing voice as the SUPEREGO, which tells the EGO or self what is right and wrong—the SUPEREGO becomes the voice of authority and morality. In exchange, he gets to keep his penis, and he is promised that eventually he will have a woman of his own.

The castration complex resolves the Oedipus complex and enables the boy to establish an ego and superego to control the id and its pleasure-seeking instincts. The boy henceforth directs his libidinal energy into creating civilization and being a non-incestuous reproductive heterosexual.

And what about the girl?

Her version of the story, according to Freud, starts with seeing a boy naked for the first time. "She sees it, and knows she is without it, and wants to have it," says Freud. Instantly, the girl feels ashamed that she doesn't have this wondrous organ—and so begins her **penis envy**. She hates herself for not having a penis and hates Mom for not having one and not giving her one. She wants to kill Mom and marry Dad in order to get his penis. At first Freud called this the "Electra Complex"; he later called it the "negative Oedipus complex."

Prior to this shocking event, the girl had been content with her clitoris, which Freud called "a miniature penis." After seeing the "real thing," however, she renounces her clitoris as inferior and renounces clitoral masturbation. She goes from active (Freud's "masculine") to passive ("feminine"), wanting to be filled with a penis rather than wield one. According to Freud, she has accepted "the fact of her castration."

Whereas the polymorphously perverse male infant becomes a properly heterosexual man relatively easily—he swears off Mom, internalizes Dad's authority, and only has to wait to get a woman of his own—the polymorphously perverse female infant has a more complex path. She has to switch her libidinal desires twice to end up as a correctly gendered heterosexual.

First, the girl has to switch from Mom as the primary object of her libidinal desires to wanting to have sex with Dad. Then she has to switch the location of her sexual pleasure, from clitoris to vagina, in order to become reproductive. In seeking to relocate her pleasure in being penetrated by a penis, she shifts from active to passive, from masculine to feminine. "The little girl has become a little woman!" declares Papa Freud.

But wait a minute! The castration complex ends the boy's Oedipus complex, pushing him to create a superego and to maintain firm boundaries between ego, id, and superego. For a girl, the Oedipus complex STARTS with "the fact of her castration." So how does it end? How do women create distinctions between ego, superego, and id?

Believe it or not, Freud isn't sure they do. Because women are already castrated, they have no compelling reason to form a superego, to internalize Dad's authority as their own voice of conscience. Thus, Freud argues, maybe women shouldn't serve as judges or elected officials because their superegos are not firmly separated and in place!

So how do women finally leave the Oedipus complex? They don't! Freud concluded that women always desire a man like Daddy. And that's why he believed so easily that the story his hysteric women patients were telling him was a fantasy rather than a reality. It was a fantasy, Freud believed, that all women share.

Although Freud admitted that he couldn't explain women, that self-knowledge never made him question his boy-based model. He assumes heterosexuality, charts how boys achieve it, and then tries to make the model fit for girls. In so doing, he admits that he doesn't really understand women's psyches much at all.

Haupter im Hieroglyphyenmutzen ("heads in hieroglyphic bonnets") is how Freud described "the riddle of femininity." Women were a text he could never read. The female mind remained, to him, "the dark continent."

Jacques Lacan

Jacques Lacan

Lacan's writings are hard to read. Like Derrida, he speaks an "interior" language—a set of terms, assumptions, and worldviews that you have to understand before you can understand his essays. For Derrida, this "interior" language was the vocabulary of Western philosophy; for Lacan, it was the

interior of psychoanalytic modes of thinking, which started with Freud.

Jacques Lacan was a French psychiatrist who worked in the 1930s and 40s with psychotic patients. In the 1950s he began to develop his own version of psychoanalysis, using structuralist linguistics to rearticulate some of Freud's basic ideas. Most notably, Lacan declared that "the unconscious is structured like a language."

Freud's idea of the unconscious was a seething mass of raging libidinal desires that were forbidden to enter into the conscious mind by the dictates of the superego. For Lacan, the unconscious is a seething mass of interlocking chains of signifiers constantly in circulation with each other, with no center to stabilize meaning: his "language" is Derrida's "différance."

Freud's conception of the unconscious split open the humanist idea of the self as a being with free will governed by rational thought. Freud revealed the dark side of the self—a side the rational self cannot control. Other writers at the end of the 19th century were exploring the same general idea through fiction: Robert Louis Stevenson's *Dr. Jekyll and Mr. Hyde* was published in 1886, the same year Freud opened his neurological clinic and began to see hysteric patients.

But Freud still thought the rational ego could conquer

the villainous unconscious. *"Wo Es war, soll Ich werden,"* he declared. "Where it (id) was, shall I (ego) be."

The project of the "talking cure," for Freud, was to bring the contents of the unconscious into consciousness, so that the rational mind, the ego, could grapple with it.

Lacan's idea of the relation between unconscious and ego, however, makes Freud's project impossible. For Lacan, the unconscious is the foundation of being. Rather than being created via the Oedipus complex, he maintained, the unconscious always already exists. The ego has to be constructed out of the endless sliding chains of signifiers by installing some kind of center that will stabilize meaning. The successful creation of the ego is marked by the subject's ability to say "I" and have that signifier designate a coherent concept of a "self"—an "I"dentity.

Both Freud and Lacan created elaborate narratives of human development. Freud's story tells how the polymorphously perverse infant navigates the incestuous perils of the Oedipus complex. The happy ending of Freud's story is the properly non-incestuous reproductive heterosexual adult who has strong boundaries between ego and unconscious, patrolled by a vigilant superego as the internalized voice of authority.

Lacan's story tells how the babbling infant misperceives itself as a "self" through identifications with others on the way to becoming a language-using subject. Lacan's happy ending is the being who uses language as if fixed meaning were possible, who is signified by "I", and who is subjected

to the commanding power of the Center.

Lacan proposes three stages of development that occur between birth and age 2-3: **the Real, the Imaginary, and the Symbolic.** You can think of these as "realms," or forms of reality, for the growing infant; each is a particular way the infant experiences the world and itself.

Human babies are born "premature"; they need constant care and nurturing in order to survive the first months (or years) of existence. Lacan, like Freud, posits the mother as the primary caregiver for the infant, the person who will supply its needs for food, warmth, and comfort.

The newborn baby in the realm of the Real is a kind of blob that eats and poops. It doesn't know anything but Need and the satisfaction of Need, according to Lacan. The baby has no conception of "self," doesn't know the boundaries of its own body, and doesn't know that the caregiver is a separate person. The baby cries, and it gets fed; the baby cries, and it gets a diaper change. Needs, within the realm of the Real, can always be satisfied.

This is the original state of "nature" that has to be broken up in order for culture to be formed. The same is true in Freud's psychoanalysis and in Lacan's: the infant must separate from its mother, form its own identity, in order to enter civilized adulthood. That separation entails some kind of LOSS. When the child knows the difference between itself and its mother, when it starts to become an individuated being, it loses its primal sense of unity (and safety/security). This is the element of the tragic built into psychoanalytic theory, whether Freudian or Lacanian: to become a civilized adult human being always entails the profound loss of an original unity, a non-differentiation, a merging with the mother.

As the baby grows, it begins to have more control over its own movements and actions, but still doesn't have a sense of "self" as the sum of all its parts. The baby works on developing "object permanence"—the ability to believe that something exists even when you can't see it. This helps the baby learn that, for instance, the foot it occasionally sees wiggling down there is its own!

Object permanence gives the baby the ability to believe that the caregiver or breast or bottle or pacifier will come back even when it's not there. This is a valuable coping skill, but one that also has existential consequences. Object permanence requires objects being absent and coming back. That means the baby has to grapple with Loss—the idea that things can go away. This gives rise to the concept of Otherness—the idea that the baby exists separately from the other beings around it.

Baby doesn't like this. It goes from expressing Needs, which can be satisfied, to making Demands, which cannot. Baby has passed out of the Real and into the Imaginary realm. Mostly, it demands not to be separate, to go back to the nice way it was before. The anxiety of loss, and the insistence of unfulfillable demands, become motives urging Baby to use language—another move away from the Real.

Because the Real is a place of fullness and completeness where there is no absence, no loss, and no Other, there is no language in the Real either. Leaving the realm of the Real means moving toward the structure of language that will enable the baby to represent selfhood with that shifty pronoun "I".

Let me explain that one. Lacan's assertion that there is no language in the Real comes from his reading of one of Freud's late essays, "Beyond the Pleasure Principle" (1920). In that work, Freud talks about watching his nephew, at the age of eighteen months, play a game with a spool tied with yarn. The kid throws the spool away and says *"Fort"* (German for "gone"); then he retrieves the spool and says *"Da"* (German for "here"). Freud figures that throwing the spool represents for the kid the absence of his mother, the fact that she goes away sometimes. He wonders why the kid would repeat the game, since the experience of Mom going away must be painful. The act of bringing the spool back, on the other hand, must be pleasurable, as it symbolizes Mom's return. Freud decides that the kid is learning mastery over the anxiety of loss by enacting his power to make the desired object return.

Lacan looks at this case and, of course, analyzes it in terms of language use. To Lacan, the important part of

Freud's description is not the act of throwing and retrieving the spool, but the kid's articulation of the act in words. The action is a repetition of loss and produces anxiety, but the mastery comes in being able to name it—to connect the action and the feelings to a specific signifier. Words are necessary only when the object they name is not there: if Mom never went away, baby would never need a signifier for her. The mastery of absence or loss is achieved through the ability to represent the lost object in language.

In the Real, then, there is no language because there is no need for language. Everything is always there, all needs are satisfiable, there is no absence or loss or "other"ness. The Real correlates with the Western philosophical ideal of Full Presence.

Because we must forever leave the realm of the Real in order to become linguistic subjects, in order to represent our world and our selves in language, the Real is always beyond language, beyond representation. Instead, we move from the Real into the Imaginary, which overlaps with the Symbolic.

Anyway, back to Baby, who has had to leave the Real behind and is learning to accept the ideas of loss, absence, and otherness. Baby has entered into the realm of the Imaginary, where the mirror phase happens and where we take our first steps into the structure of language in the Symbolic.

In his 1949 essay "The Mirror Stage as Formative of the

Function of the I as Revealed in Psychoanalytic Experience," Lacan examines "the formation of the I as we experience it in psychoanalysis. It is an experience that leads us to oppose any philosophy directly issuing from the *cogito.*"

The *cogito,* remember, is Rene Descartes' statement "I think therefore I am." Descartes identified the being that thinks as "I" and assumed that the "I" is stable, autonomous, and conscious; he doesn't problematize the meaning of "I". Lacan's argument, by contrast, focuses on the *instability* of the pronoun "I". He says we have to learn that "I" designates the thing called "self" and that we do so via the mirror stage.

Lacan's essay compares a six-month-old chimpanzee with a six-month-old human baby. While the chimp is superior to the baby in "instrumental intelligence"—the ability to manipulate objects in its environment—the chimp isn't interested in the image it sees when looking in a mirror. Like most animals, the chimp will see an image and not identify the image as itself; it loses interest after a while. (Try this with a dog or cat. The animal will sniff the mirror, maybe paw at it, but pretty quickly gets bored because the image is not "real" to it.)

The six-month-old child, however, is "jubilant" in relation to the mirror; Lacan emphasizes the baby's excitement in seeing the image. The human infant, according to Lacan, is experiencing the mirror image differently than an animal does: the baby has an *"aha-erlebnis,"* a moment of epiphany or revelation, in interacting with the mirror image. This epiphany, for Lacan, is the moment when the baby sees itself

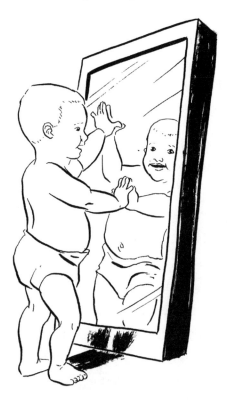

as a whole being; indeed it sees its whole world (gestalt) reflected back to it as containing that whole being.

The "aha moment" of the mirror stage is the infant's first moment of **identification**. With the help of caregivers around it, it learns that that image is called "you." The infant sees itself as an image, an *imago*, and starts the process of identifying with that image. This, for Lacan, is the first experience of the ego, the I, the self.

The jubilant assumption of his specular image ...
would seem to exhibit ... the symbolic matrix in
which the I is precipitated in a primordial form,

before it is objectified in the dialectic of identifica-
tion with the other, and before language restores
to it, in the universal, its function as subject.

In other words, the "aha" of the mirror stage is the first appearance of the possibility of self, of I, before the infant fully inhabits the structure of language in which "I" functions as a subject pronoun.

This first identification with the mirror image, with an *imago* perceived as a totality, unitary and total—with all body parts connected into a single whole—"situates the agency of the ego, before its social determination, in a fictional direction." The emerging self will take as its internalized model the whole self it sees in the mirror. In addition, this self will internalize the whole gestalt perceived in the mirror (including caregivers, toys, what have you) as the place in which it becomes whole.

We are born premature, argues Lacan, and we experience ourselves as fragmented, in pieces, until this moment of seeing the imago as whole. Then, for the first time, the infant perceives an image of itself that looks like all the people around it.

The mirror stage is a drama whose internal thrust
is precipitated from insufficiency to anticipation
and which manufactures for the subject, caught
up in the lure of spatial identification, the suc-
cession of phantasies that extends from the frag-

mented body-image to a form of its totality that I
shall call orthopedic....

What the baby sees is "orthopedic"—seeing itself as whole while still experiencing itself as fragmented, leads the baby toward identification with the complete image. This, Lacan argues, is a misperception or a mis-identification that will lead the baby to become a self that always feels less than the image of wholeness it has seen.

The moment of the "mirror stage" provides the pattern for the rest of the baby's growth and identification—a moment when the baby sees an image and misrecognizes that image as itself. This misrecognition—*meconnaissance*—lies at the core of Lacan's idea of the self or ego. In Lacan's terms, this misrecognition creates the "armor"—an illusion or misperception of wholeness, integration, and totality that surrounds and protects the fragmented body. To

Lacan, the ego, self, or "I"dentity is always on some level a FANTASY, an identification with an external image and not an internal sense of separate whole identity.

The fact that the *"aha-erlebnis"* moment happens while looking in a mirror (or any reflective surface, such as water) emphasizes the centrality of vision to Lacan's idea of the ego. The self that is built through the moment at the mirror is a specular self.

Lacan is big on the word "other." He insists that the infant learns the idea of "otherness" long before the idea of "self," and that the "self" built through internalizing the mirror's image creates "self" AS "other." The idea of "other" contains the ideas of "lack" and "loss" and "absence," all of which, within a psychoanalytic framework, are necessities of linguistic selfhood. Using signifiers to represent things reliably is compensation for having lost the original unity of the Real.

Lacan highlights the importance of the idea of "other" by naming the center of his Symbolic Order "the Other." He distinguishes between the capital-o Other as center and small-o others who inhabit subject positions within the Symbolic Order and who are subjected to the governance of the center.

Lacan looks at the *fort/da* game played by Freud's nephew and sees the kid using linguistic signifiers to negotiate the idea of absence. The spool serves as an *"objet*

petit a" or *"objet petit autre"*—a small-o other that the child can manipulate rather than the big-O Other to which the child is subject.

Lacan has lots of names for the center of the Symbolic Order:

> The Other
>
> The Law
>
> The Law of the Father
>
> The Name of the Father
>
> The Phallus

You can tell from these names that Freud is alive in Lacan's version of psychoanalysis. Lacan takes Freud's Oedipal images of the power of the penis and the father's angry authority as descriptions of the center of the Symbolic. For Lacan, it is the force or power that serves as a Transcendental Signified, a control center for maintaining a stable structure of language and the subject positions it creates.

The center is the place of complete fullness, the place that would fulfill the desires created by absence, loss, lack, and otherness. Everyone wants to be the center, or to be what the center wants, but no one can be.

Calling the center "the Phallus" points to Freud's enshrinement of the penis as the only organ worth having. It may be possible that beings with penises (mis)identify with the Phallus as center more easily than do beings without penises! Certainly gender plays a role in Lacan's Symbolic Order, though not (thankfully) the same restrictive role that it played in Freud.

Lacan talks about gender in a 1966 essay titled "The Agency of the Letter in the Unconscious." In it he includes two drawings. One is of the word "Tree" over a picture of a tree—the basic Saussurean concept of signifier (word) over signified (object). The other drawing is of two identical doors (the signifieds), with a different word over each. One says "Ladies," and the other says "Gentlemen." Lacan explains,

> *A train arrives at a station. A little boy and a little girl, brother and sister, are seated in a compartment face to face next to the window through which the buildings along the station platform can be seen passing as the train pulls to a stop. "Look," says the brother, "We're at Ladies!" "Idiot!" replies his sister. "Can't you see we're at Gentlemen?"*

This anecdote shows how boys and girls enter the Symbolic order—the structure of language—differently. In Lacan's view, each child can see only the signifier of the

other gender; the individual child constructs its worldview, its understanding of the relation between signifier and signified in naming locations, as the consequence of seeing an "other." As Lacan puts it, "For these children, Ladies and Gentlemen will be henceforth two countries toward which each of their souls will strive on divergent wings...." Each child, each sex has a particular position within the Symbolic order; from that position, each sex can see (or signify) only the otherness of the other sex.

You might take Lacan's drawing of the two doors literally: these are the doors, with their gender distinctions, through which each child must pass in order to enter into the Symbolic realm.

As you may have gathered by now, feminist theorists have had a lot to say about psychoanalytic theory! So let's move on.

Chapter 5
FEMINIST, GENDER, AND QUEER THEORIES

Simone de Beauvoir

Twentieth-century Western feminist theory might be said to begin with Simone de Beauvoir's analysis of gender inequality in *The Second Sex* (1949). De Beauvoir argued in particular with Freud's conclusion that anatomy is destiny, seeing gender relations as products of social relations rather than as biology. One is not born a woman, de Beauvoir argued—one becomes a woman. Her perspective was taken up by subsequent feminist theorists, including the American Kate Millet, whose *Sexual Politics* (1971) gained media attention as part of the "women's liberation" movement. Both de Beauvoir and Millet grappled specifically with the sexism of Freudian psychoanalysis.

In addition to critiquing Freud, Millet analyzed the issue of gender in literary studies. Like many other feminist literary critics, she asked why the existing "canon" of great writers included no women. Feminist critics examined the depiction of women in literature, art, and popular culture; other feminist critics recovered "lost" women writers and

Susan Gubar

republished their texts. In *The Madwoman in the Attic* (1980), Sandra Gilbert and Susan Gubar asked if the pen is a metaphoric penis and, in doing so, helped bring gender to center stage as an important analytical field in literary and cultural studies.

These forms of feminist literary theory examined gender relations historically and psychologically, while feminist theorists in Paris were, with their male colleagues, discussing gender within a poststructuralist framework. The authors represented in *New French Feminisms* (1980) followed Lacan and Derrida in positing that the centered structure of language they describe is gendered.

Poststructuralist feminist theory begins with the assumption that "gender" exists as sets of signifiers whose supposed signifieds are sexually dimorphic human bodies. The connections between these signifiers and their signifieds are, of course, arbitrary and can be dislocated or deconstructed. Lipstick signifies femininity, but anybody can wear it.

If "language speaks us," then it must speak gender. Poststructuralist feminist theory examines how.

Most languages already have gender built in to their structure; English is one of the few languages in which nouns do not have specific gender. But that's not quite what poststructuralist feminist theories are about.

Let's go back to Lacan and his image of the train pulling into the station. From where the girl sits, all she can see is the door that says "Gentlemen." From the boy's perspective, all he can see is "Ladies." Lacan uses this image to discuss the idea of desire: desire is always desire of the Other, to be where the Other is.

We can also use those images as doors to the Symbolic Order—to the realm of stable language controlled by the center.

Imagine the Symbolic as a giant auditorium. You have a ticket that assigns you a seat; that is your subject position, from which perspective you view what happens on stage. The tickets marked "Gentlemen" put you in different seats than the tickets marked "Ladies." (Other forms of social discrimination, such as sexuality, race, and social class, can also be marked on the tickets.)

Once seated in your proper position within the Symbolic, you can use language as if each word has a definitive knowable definable meaning. You can speak as a subject within the Cartesian rational philosophical tradition and say "I" with impunity. But speaking as if words have fixed meaning comes with a price: you have to follow the rules of the Center. And in Lacan's Symbolic Order, the Center is decidedly masculine: the Phallus, the Name-of-the-Father, the Law-of the-Father. This centered system is logocentric and phallocentric—or, in short, **phallogocentric**.

The seats for Gentlemen are up front, close to the phallic center; the seats for Ladies are in the rear, farther away from the center. Thus, the position "woman" in the Symbolic is aligned with the idea of Lack, following Freud's idea that the female is a castrated male. Lacan argues that any speaking subject is already constituted by Lack, regardless of gender: to enter the Symbolic is to embrace language as compensation for the loss of the Real. The ability to represent the world through words, for Lacan, is based on our complete exclusion from a paradisiacal original unity where there was no lack, no desire, no language. In this sense, the maternal body, the female body, is also excluded from the Symbolic. And this raises the question of whether the subject position "woman" can speak at all—or does anyone speaking within the phallogocentric Symbolic Order speak as "man"?

Hélène Cixous

Hélène Cixous

The French feminist author and critic Hélène Cixous introduces the concept of *l'ecriture feminine,* or feminine writing, which she hopes will deconstruct the binary oppositions held together by the Phallus. Cixous and other feminist theorists, such as Julia Kristeva and Luce Irigaray, posit that the position of woman/feminine/otherness is ungoverned by the power of the phallic center. A subject speaking or writing from the margins of the Symbolic—from the back rows that are not as firmly held in place—disrupts the coherence, seamlessness, and stability of the phallogocentric Symbolic Order. To speak or write from the "feminine" position creates a "rupture," in the Derridean sense, where fixed meaning becomes destabilized.

At the beginning of her best-known essay, "The Laugh of the Medusa" (1975), Cixous announces: "I shall speak about women's writing, about *what it will do.* Woman must write her self: must write about women and bring women to writing." Cixous is quite serious in claiming a feminine writing, which she opposes to masculine writing:

I mean it when I speak of male writing. I maintain unequivocally that there is such a thing as marked writing; that, until now, far more extensively and repressively than is ever suspected or admitted, writing has been run by a libidinal and cultural— hence political, typically masculine—economy.

She refuses to define what *l'ecriture feminine* is exactly, because

It is impossible to define a feminine practice of writing, and this is an impossibility that will remain, for this practice can never be theorized, enclosed, encoded—which doesn't mean that it doesn't exist. But it will always surpass the discourse that regulates the phallogocentric system; it does and will take place in areas other than those subordinated to philosophico-theoretical domination. It will be conceived of only by subjects who are breakers of automatisms, by peripheral figures that no authority can ever subjugate.

Cixous describes *l'ecriture feminine* rather than defining it. She is careful not to say what it looks like, since "looking like" is at the heart of the misperception of self in the Mirror Stage, the first step into the Symbolic. Rather, her metaphors invoke a different register of experience than the visual or the verbal: *l'ecriture feminine* is milk, it's song, something with rhythm and pulse but no words, something connected with bodies and with bodies' beats and movements, but not with representational language. Woman writes "in white ink," Cixous declares, using the image of breast milk to create a reunion with the maternal body forbidden in the phallogocentric Symbolic Order.

One of Cixous' main ideas is that the Symbolic Order and its phallogocentric ideology depend on excluding anything that is not defined in relation to itself. Within the Symbolic, where you need a phallic center to stabilize meaning, "female" must necessarily be defined by lack, as "not male," by absence rather than presence. In this logic, female is always "other" than male, defined by what he has and she lacks rather than by anything intrinsic to herself.

Cixous uses the word "feminine" to invoke the binary opposition favoring the masculine, but also to refer to something that exists outside or beyond the phallogocentric

Symbolic and its binary oppositions. She associates this "feminine" with the maternal body and other experiences that "escape discourse," that cannot be represented in language.

Chief among the experiences that escape the structuring rules of the center is what Lacan calls *jouissance,* the French word for orgasm. In this context, the word means a form of pleasure that goes beyond language, beyond discourse, something that can't be expressed in words or in the structure of language. More specifically, the form of pleasure that escapes or exceeds the rules and structures held in place by the Phallus is a specifically feminine pleasure, a feminine *jouissance,* which is unrepresentable in language. In fact, it works to disrupt language, interrupt representation, disturb the linear flow of language and narrative. This *jouissance* can also be considered a type of deconstruction, as it shakes up the fixity and stability of language (where meaning is held in place by the Phallus) and puts signifiers into play, making them slippery and indeterminate.

To understand this, we have to look back at the mess Freud made in trying to explain how girls become properly heterosexual. His model requires girls to make two switches in their Oedipal phase: to switch objects, from the mother's body to the father's penis; and to switch erotic zones, from clitoral stimulation to vaginal, as a source of pleasure. The active masculine girl thus becomes the passive feminine woman.

In this model, poststructuralist feminists point out, there is no such thing as female sexuality per se. Passively waiting to be filled by a penis makes no reference to anything intrinsic to the female body or to the anatomy of female sexual pleasure.

So Cixous declares that feminine *jouissance*, like feminine writing, lies beyond the control of the Symbolic and its Phallus, free to play or disrupt its structures.

> *A feminine text cannot fail to be more than subversive. It is volcanic; as it is written it brings about an upheaval of the old property crust, carrier of masculine investments; there's no other way. There's no room for her if she's not a he. If she's a her-she, it's in order to smash everything, to shatter the framework of institutions, to blow up the law, to break up the "truth" with laughter.*

Cixous calls for women to write their own texts of *jouissance*—an experience that creates "forms much more beautiful than those which are put up in frames and sold for a stinking fortune."

Text: my body—shot through with streams of song; I don't mean the overbearing, clutchy "mother" but rather what touches you, the voice that affects you, fills your breast with an urge to come to language and launch your force; the rhythm that laughs you; the intimate recipient who makes all metaphors possible and desirable; body (body? Bodies?) no more describable than God, the soul, or the Other; that part of you that leaves a space between yourself and urges you to inscribe in language your woman's style.

There are two levels on which *l'ecriture feminine* will be transformative, Cixous argues: a literal, individual level and a metaphoric, structural level. On the first, the individual woman must write herself, must discover for herself what her body feels like and how to write about that body in language. Specifically, women must find their own sexuality, one that is rooted solely in their own bodies, and find ways to write about that pleasure, that *jouissance.*

On the second level, when women speak/write their own bodies, the structure of language itself will change. As women become active subjects, not just beings passively acted upon, their position as subject in language will shift. Women who write—if they don't merely reproduce the phallogocentric system of stable ordered meaning which already exists (and excludes them)—will be creating a new signifying system. This system may have built into it far more play and fluidity than the existing rigid phallogocentric symbolic order. "Beware, my friend," Cixous writes toward the end of the essay, "of the signifier that would take you back to the authority of a signified!"

The woman who speaks, Cixous says, and who does not reproduce the representational stability of the Symbolic order, will not speak in linear fashion; she will not "make sense" in any currently existing form. *L'ecriture feminine,* like feminine speech, will not be objective/objectifiable; it will erase the divisions between speech and text, between order and chaos, between sense and nonsense. In this way, *l'ecriture feminine* will be an inherently deconstructive language.

Although Cixous insists that *l'ecriture feminine* is female writing, connected to female bodies and female sexual experiences, she also argues that men must write men. By separating from the maternal body, men within the Symbolic learn to leave their own bodies behind, in favor of the rationality of the Cartesian mind. "Men still have everything to say about their sexuality, and everything to write." Male bodies are more than just penises, just as female bodies are more than just vaginas.

Cixous' essay conjures the image of Medusa, the Greek gorgon who had snakes for hair and whose gaze could turn men into stone. Medusa represents the darkness and danger inherent in women from the psychoanalytic perspective. Perseus, as masculine hero, must find a way to kill her.

For Cixous, Medusa is the woman/mother/other outside the Symbolic, a figure that terrifies and disrupts the phallogocentric order. She sees Perseus trembling, unable to face her gaze because she threatens to take away his privileged relationship with the Phallus. He has one penis— she has many, writhing in plain sight on top of her head.

If we look directly at Medusa, Cixous urges, we will see that "she's not deadly. She's beautiful and she's laughing." Medusa is laughing at the ridiculousness that patriarchy has produced and that Freudian and Lacanian psychoanalysis have explained and solidified. How silly to value one scrap of flesh over another. She laughs with joy at writing that plays, that erupts, that slips and slides.

There is no "truth" in such writing. Rather, this laughter, this writing, this *jouissance* works to create an "Other love," a new love that "dares for the other, wants the other, makes dizzying, precipitous flights between knowledge and invention." This is a desire that gives rather than lacks. "It's not impossible, and this is what nourishes life—a love that has no commerce with the apprehensive desire that provides against the lack and stultifies the strange; a love that rejoices in the exchange that multiplies." And so, say Cixous,

> *When I write, it's everything that we don't know we can be that is written out of me, without exclusions, without stipulation, and everything we will be calls us to the unflagging, intoxicating, unappeasable search for love. In one another we will never be lacking.*

Judith Butler and "Gender Trouble"

Judith Butler's poststructuralist theories provide a bridge between feminist theory and queer theory. In her book *Gender Trouble: Feminism and the Subversion of Identity* (1990), Butler deconstructs the binary male/female and masculine/feminine by means of **phenomenology**.

Judith Butler

Another big word, but don't panic! Phenomenology is the study of consciousness from the first-person point of view—how we experience the world. Butler argues that phenomenol-

ogy is a particularly rich way to think about theater and performance, because phenomenology "seeks to explain the mundane way in which social agents *constitute* social reality through language, gesture, and all manner of symbolic social sign."

An actor in a play is both repeating/reciting a script that's already written AND enacting that script for the first time, as an original and unique performance. Social reality within a play is created for the audience by the interaction of the preexisting script and the specific moment of the performance of that script. The idea here is that, in phenomenological analysis, an actor is both constructive and constructed—the actor shapes the role, but the role shapes the actor. This gives the actor more agency than Lacan's linguistically imprisoned subject.

Butler uses this idea to discuss how gender is created and maintained. She quotes Simone de Beauvoir's statement that "one is not born a woman, one becomes a woman." Biological sex is not sufficient to explain the creation of "woman," the creation of gender roles and expectations.

Let's unpack that a little. In Western culture, we recognize only two sexes: male and female. But there are at least six markers of biological sex: external genitalia (penis

or vagina); internal reproductive organs (testes or ovaries); sex chromosomes (XX or XY); sex hormones (testosterone or estrogen); and skeletal structure (the pelvis, for example). There may also be sex differences in brain structure and/ or brain chemistry. The point is, Western culture reduces the relevant markers to a binary opposition—you ARE male or female. And if your anatomy doesn't conform to that binary structure (say you have a penis *and* ovaries, for example) then your anatomy is wrong and will be surgically or chemically corrected so you do conform to the binary male/female model.

In Western culture, biological sex is supposed to determine gender and sexuality. If you are a male, you should be masculine, and if you are male and masculine you will be heterosexual. Likewise, if you are a female, you should be feminine, and thus heterosexual with the masculine male. Anything that disrupts that order—such as having a penis but wearing a dress—makes you "queer." Butler challenges this biological sequence by pointing out that bodies are both a biological "fact" and a locus of social meanings; gender is the cultural significance of the sexed body.

Butler relies on the French phenomenologist Maurice Merleau-Ponty in exploring "the body" as sets of possibilities to be continually realized, rather than as something essential, predetermined, or given. Bodies, from this perspective, are always **enacted:** the inhabitant of a particular body takes up and performs historically determined roles or positions. For example, if gender rules said that masculine men wear giant powdered wigs, beauty spots, and satin knee pants, then male bodies will perform that masculine role.

Butler argues that one "does" one's body—that one performs one's bodily identities, such as gender. Gender is a *corporeal style,* an "act" that is both intentional and performative. The subject, according to Butler, is always in the process of embodying possible roles, identities, or positions. A culture provides certain possibilities for gender roles, and subjects then reaffirm and create those roles by enacting them.

To be male or female is a biological fact (though that formulation can be problematic, as we've seen with the multiple signifiers of sex). To be a woman, de Beauvoir and Butler agree, is a performance.

Butler talks about the "rituals, gestures, and enactments" that create and conform to some historical idea of "woman."

To create or "do" "woman," one enacts (or is compelled to enact) certain culturally available gender "scripts." Gender is signified through a subject's body by the repetition of these enactments—to continuously and repeatedly materialize one's "self" in obedience to some historically defined (i.e., culturally constructed) possibility.

Butler chides poststructuralist critics who see gender as a set of rules and sanctions imposed on a passive sexed body. Bodies do not "pre-exist" cultural codes, she says; nor do cultural codes completely circumscribe or define individual bodily performances. In insisting that gender is ALWAYS a performance, Butler enables us to think about both the imposed aspect of gender—the already-written cultural scripts of gender-appropriate behavior—and about the improvisational, individual creation of gender, which exists in each performance of a script. The gendered subject, she concludes, is an **actor**, in the sense of theatrical performer, who plays the same role over and over but does so with individual and unpredictable nuances.

Gender as performance is always drag.

Drag is a cultural phenomenon from the LGBT or queer community. Originally, the term "drag queen" referred to a man who dressed as a woman, often with highly exaggerated feminine gender characteristics. Butler points out, however, that the transvestite who entertains you on the stage becomes a threat or danger when s/he sits next to you on a bus. The transvestite on stage or bus is performing gender, but on the bus there are no boundaries or rules about the limits of the performance, as there are in the theater. The transvestite on the bus threatens to expose all gender categories as social constructs and all gender enactments as performative. The normative functions of gender regulation make the other bus riders wonder, "What are you, *really?*"

Two final points:

First, Butler concludes,

genders ... can be neither true nor false, neither real nor apparent. And yet, one is compelled to live in a world in which genders constitute univocal signifiers in which gender is stabilized, polarized, rendered discrete and intractable. In effect, gender is made to comply with a model of truth or falsity which not only contradicts its own performative fluidity, but serves a social policy of gender regulation and control.

Second, Butler points out, gender scripts are enforced by systems of reward and punishment. You can think of your own examples of how nonconformity to some existing gender paradigm can have personal and social consequences.

Queer Theory

"Broadly speaking," wrote Annamarie Jagose in *Queer Theory: An Introduction* (1996),

> *queer describes those gestures or analytical models which dramatise incoherencies in the allegedly stable relations between chromosomal sex, gender, and sexual desire. Resisting that model of stability—which claims heterosexuality as its origin, when it is more properly its effect—queer focuses on mismatches between sex, gender, and desire. Institutionally, queer has been associated most prominently with lesbian and gay subjects, but its analytic framework also includes such topics as cross-dressing, hermaphroditism, gender ambiguity, and gender-corrective surgery. Whether as transvestite performance or academic deconstruction, queer locates and exploits the incoherencies in those three terms which stabilise heterosexuality. Demonstrating the impossibility of any "natural" sexuality, it calls into question even such apparently unproblematic terms as "man" and "woman."*

Gender performance is dangerous not only because it exposes the artificiality of supposedly biological gender roles, but because it also exposes the artificiality of the

119

sexual identity that supposedly accompanies gender conformity. Queer theorists examine and question what Gayle Rubin has dubbed the "sex/gender system," which equates body sex with proper gender identity, and proper gender identity with proper sexual identity. Other queer theorists, such as the poet Adrienne Rich, have called this reinforcement "compulsory heterosexuality."

In her 1975 essay "The Traffic in Women: Notes on the 'Political Economy' of Sex," Rubin examines one of the main premises of Lévi-Strauss's structural anthropology: "the exchange of women." The need for exogamy, Rubin contends, creates a system in which women are exchanged between groups of men but have no rights to dispose of themselves, to be "selves" themselves. Compulsory heterosexuality works to turn female sexuality into a commodity, something that can be exchanged for something else. Women no longer own themselves, but become objects to circulate like goods.

For Lévi-Strauss, this was theory. For Rubin, it is a crucial aspect of patriarchy. For many thousands of women around the world, it is the inescapable reality of sexual slavery.

Luce Irigaray

Luce Irigaray, a lesbian poststructuralist feminist theorist, sees lesbian sexuality as a means of breaking up the "exchange of women." Using Marxist and psychoanalytic theory, Irigaray argues that lesbian sexuality has no "exchange value" because it is not involved with reproduction. Like Cixous, she celebrates a sexuality that is about female pleasure, not about penises or kinship systems. "The interplay of desire among women's bodies, sexes, and speech is inconceivable in the dominant socio-cultural economy," says Irigaray. And she elaborates:

Female homosexuality exists, nevertheless. But it is admitted only in as far as it is prostituted to the fantasies of men. Goods can only enter into relations under the surveillance of their "guardians." It would be out of the question for them to go to the "market" alone, to profit from their own value, to talk to each other, to desire each other, without the control of the selling-buying-consuming subjects. And their relations must be relations of rivalry in the interest of tradesmen.

But what if the "goods" refused to go to market? What if they maintained among themselves "another" kind of trade?

Irigaray expands her analysis of lesbian sexuality in *This Sex Which Is Not One* (1985), agreeing with Cixous' argument that Freud's version of female sexuality has nothing to do with women's bodies or pleasures at all. In Freud's model, she writes,

> *woman's erogenous zones never amount to anything but a clitoris-sex that is not comparable to the noble phallic organ, or a hole-envelope that serves to sheathe and massage the penis in intercourse.*

Instead, Irigaray offers a female eroticism foreign to the dominant phallic economy:

> *In order to touch himself, man needs an instrument: his hand, a woman's body, language.... As for woman, she touches herself in and of herself without any need for mediation.... She "touches herself" all the time, and moreover no one can forbid her to do so, for her genitals are formed of two lips in continuous contact. Thus, within herself, she is already two—but not divisible into one(s)—that caress each other.*

Irigaray points out that psychoanalytic models privilege vision over all the other senses, regarding female bodies as lacking because there is "nothing to see." Au contraire, she says—women have sex organs more or less everywhere, in an eroticism of touch and plurality that cannot be reduced to one single thing, like a phallus. Like Cixous, she insists that feminine sexuality is intimately tied to feminine language; feminine writing is multiple, fluid, and ultimately, deconstructive.

Michel Foucault

One more important queer theorist: Michel Foucault. Volume 1 of his *History of Sexuality* (published as *La Volonte de savoir* in France in 1976) opened a new area of investigation of sexuality, or sexual identity, as socially and historically constructed.

Foucault argues that sexuality as an identity category—a way you describe your core self, who you are—emerged during the mid-Victorian era in Western culture as the result of social regimes designed to regulate sex. Rather than being repressed, as Freud had thought, sex was everywhere. Freud's own writings are part of what Foucault might agree to call the "discursive construction of sexuality" in the 19th and 20th centuries.

Historically, Foucault posits, there was no such thing as "sexuality" until the mid-19th century. Not that there wasn't sex—people had all kinds of sex all kinds of ways—but a sex act didn't constitute an identity category. In plain English, you could fuck a sheep but that didn't make you a sheepfucker. Sexual behavior morphed from a policeable act to an identity, part of the essential self so beloved of humanism. And the social regulation of sexuality—enforcing the power relations of the binary oppositions—became a matter of internalization and correction.

Homosexuality, at this time, was established as a deviant identity, an undesirable subject position, through legal, medical, theological, and psychological discourses. Where "sodomy" is against the law, the homosexual becomes a criminal; where sodomy is deemed unnatural, the homosexual becomes sick or unhealthy. The dominant cultural modes of enforcement worked to imprison, correct, or "cure" the deviant side of the binary opposition in hopes of eliminating it. Foucault, along with other poststructuralists, points out that the structure of the binary opposition requires that both terms be present: the concept of "normal" requires the concept of "deviant" for each to exist. Discourses and practices that try to "correct" or eliminate the deviance of homosexuality actually construct and reinforce that deviance.

Chapter 6
IDEOLOGY AND DISCOURSE

What is "ideology"? An ideology is a belief system. Synonyms might include "worldview," "paradigm," "perspective," "truth," "reality," and "why things are the way they are."

Ideology is how a society thinks about itself, the forms of social consciousness that exist at any particular moment. Ideologies supply all the terms and assumptions and frameworks that individuals use to understand their culture; they supply all the things that people believe in and then act on.

For Karl Marx, and for Marxist theory in general, ideologies were the superstructure that was built on the foundation of the economic base. Belief systems were

generated to explain and justify modes of production. Think, for example, of slavery in the United States. As a means of production, slavery organized every aspect of Southern society and fostered ideologies that supported the institution of slavery itself. Every Sunday from the pulpit, slaveholders and slaves alike could hear that the Bible sanctified slavery, and thus believe that the slave system was divinely ordained.

Literature became an important place where those belief systems were articulated and debated. Abraham Lincoln blamed Harriet Beecher Stowe's novel *Uncle Tom's Cabin* (1852) for helping start the Civil War.

In classical Marxism, literature was seen as part of the ideological superstructure of any particular economic system. Thus, early Marxist literary theory examined how a work of literature was determined by a mode of production. Friedrich Engels, Marx's co-author of *The Communist Manifesto* (1848), said that literature promoted "false consciousness"—novels especially worked to create a worldview that supported capitalist values. Later Marxists, such as Pierre Macheray in France, argued that literature was not just a transparent vehicle for the beliefs of the dominant class; literature did not just reflect social conditions and beliefs. For these theorists, literature was a venue where ideologies could be challenged or rewritten.

For other Marxists, including the Germans Bertolt Brecht and Walter Benjamin, literature works much as any ideology does—by signifying the imaginary ways in which people perceive the real world. Fiction, in particular, uses language to signify what it feels like to live in particular conditions, rather than using language to give a rational analysis of those conditions. Thus, they believed, literature helps to *create* experience, not just reflect it. Literature for these critics is relatively autonomous, both of other ideological forms and of the economic system. The social functions of literature—how it makes its audiences think and feel and believe and act—are a much richer ground for analysis than any kind of deterministic link between economic base and literary creation.

Louis Althusser: Ideology and Ideological State Apparatuses

Louis Althusser

The French philosopher Louis Althusser, writing in the early 1960s, applied structuralism to Marxism, reconceptualizing Marx's 19th-century humanist "self" as the subject constructed in and by language. Marx had imagined an autonomous self with free will whose fundamental humanity is doubly alienated by the capitalist mode of production. Althusser imagines networks of ideologies that produce subject positions inhabited by individuals. These subject positions are

127

generated by ideologies themselves, according to Althusser; they are part of the overall structure of ideology.

Let's unpack that. Althusser argues that ideology, in any culture, is the structural position for ideas and belief systems. Structuralism, remember, in its search for human universals, argued that every human culture has certain basic structural arrangements: a signifying system or language, a kinship system, an economic system, and a system of governance. The system of governance produces and enforces the rules that the culture follows, and ideology is a crucial part of that system. Ideology is the expression of the logic that the rules of a culture follow; it explains why you do what you do.

Althusser examines the modern nation-state as it existed in Europe during the 20th century, suspicious of the powers of the State to terrorize its people (as evidenced by Hitler and Stalin). How does the State control its citizens and get them to act according to its agenda? Why don't people resist, rebel, revolt? This is a central question for theorists investigating ideology and discourse—the means by which the governing power (the State) articulates and enforces both the rules by which people must act and the ideas that make them believe in those rules.

Althusser says that the State has two primary mechanisms for getting people to follow the rules and behave correctly: Repressive State Apparatuses (RSAs) and Ideological State Apparatuses (ISAs).

Repressive State Apparatuses are the material forces a government has at its disposal to physically control people, including the police and the army. An RSA enforces the rules through the threat of physical confinement (imprisonment); RSAs are linked to judicial and political systems via courts and laws, also maintained by RSAs.

Ideological State Apparatuses are the nonphysical forces a government has to make you believe in the rules it wants you to follow. ISAs include institutions like public schools, which indoctrinate kids into the belief systems the State upholds. The goal of an ISA is to teach you how to think so that you will behave and follow the rules, thus reducing the need for RSAs.

Did you have to say the Pledge of Allegiance when you were in school? Did you have to stand with your hand over your heart as you recited the words? That's a material ritual that enacts and embodies the ideas of the State.

Althusser, as he tries to reconcile Marx's materialism with structuralism's abstractions, insists that beliefs are always tied to practices, and vice versa. Beliefs, he argues, have currency only if they are enacted. Thus, every belief is tied to a material practice (an action), and every action occurs due to a belief, conscious or unconscious.

This is one of the central ideas of Althusser's best-known essay, "Ideology and Ideological State Apparatuses" (1970): Ideology has a material existence in the practices of subjects. There is no practice except by and in an ideology, he declares. There is no ideology except by the subject and for the subject who practices it. The subject, the self, the individual, the citizen is "the constitutive category of all ideology," and the primary function of ideology is "to constitute concrete individuals as subjects."

Althusser's essay investigates the mechanisms through which a subject comes to believe in a particular ideology, and then to enact the rituals of that ideology. He calls this process one of **interpellation**, or "hailing"—like you would hail a cab. An ideology calls to you, Althusser says, hoping you will pull over and take it in. "Hey you!" it hollers, hoping you'll stop and say, "Who, me?"

In interacting with an ideology, a person feels named or seen—*"You mean me?"* If the ideology succeeds in naming the person correctly—if the person recognizes him/herself in what the ideology is saying, in accordance with how the subject has previously been interpellated into other ideologies—then the person becomes a subject of the ideology, believing in it and practicing it.

This process of interpellation, or hailing, happens all the time with any kind of ideology. Perhaps it's most obvious in advertising, which constantly and aggressively addresses a "you" that names its subject position and seeks out people to inhabit it.

"Do YOU want the perfect in-home workout? Do YOU want abs and buns of steel?" If you see this commercial and answer "Yes, I do!" then you become a subject of its ideology—the idea that everyone wants to be fit, buff, and ripped. The perfect body is the center of the structure of this ideology. If you believe this ideology, you'll recognize yourself in the "Hey you" and you'll act in accordance with it and buy the product they're selling.

The interpellation of individuals as subjects presupposes the existence of a kind of center, in the Derridean and Lacanian sense—a god-term or Other, which Althusser calls the Subject.

Althusser gives a Biblical example: God calls Moses by name, and Moses says *"It is I"*—God calls Moses, names him as His subject, and Moses says yes, that's me. Moses thus becomes a subject through a relation with the Subject (God), and is subjected to the rules of the Subject.

The Subject needs subjects just as much as the subjects need the Subject. Althusser describes a mirroring process between Subject and subject, using the Lacanian concept of "specularity" to describe a mutual process of recognition and double-mirroring. (Althusser was a big fan of Lacan and wrote extensively about Freudian and Lacanian psychoanalysis.)

> *The duplicate mirror structure of ideology en-*
> *sures simultaneously:*
> *1) the interpellation of "individuals" as subjects;*
> *2) their subjection to the Subject;*
> *3) the mutual recognition of subjects and Subject,*

the subjects' recognition of each other, and finally
the subject's recognition of himself;
4) the absolute guarantee that everything really
is so, and that on condition that the subjects rec-
ognize what they are and behave accordingly, ev-
erything will be all right: Amen—"so be it."
—Louis Althusser, "Ideology and Ideological
State Apparatuses"

Within ideology as centered by the Subject, subjects "work by themselves": they know the rules and follow them because they identify with (and within) the system that the rules articulate, founded on a mirrored identification with the Subject. (In case that identification doesn't work—if a subject doesn't behave according to the rules—the RSAs are there to enforce them.)

Ideologies are everywhere; we are constantly soaking in them. Althusser might rewrite Derrida's insistence that there is no outside the text as there is no outside of ideologies. Just as you can't think outside of language because you can't think *without* language, so, too, you can't think outside of ideologies because you can't think without them.

We are always subjects, constantly practicing the rituals of ideological recognition. In this sense, the writing I am currently performing, and the reading you are currently performing (though they don't both happen at the same time), are rituals of ideological recognition. You, the reader, recognize me, the author, just as I recognize you by naming you "reader."

And this is where literature comes in. From a Marxist perspective, literature is a locus of ideology, a mechanism by which ideologies are formulated and distributed. We saw this earlier in the didactic approach to literature, which argued that the ideas contained in literary works can indeed influence the thought and behavior of their readers. We also saw it in early Marxist literary theory, which held that literature merely reproduces the interests of the ruling class.

Literature, particularly fiction, can certainly become the tool of the State. When it does, we call it "propaganda," noting that its literary value diminishes as its political agenda becomes obvious. All literature, however, conveys ideologies in the points of view of various characters and narrators as well as in the stylistic choices an author makes.

Mikhail Bakhtin, "Discourse in the Novel"

From the poststructuralist point of view, we are always already subjects within language. We cannot speak outside of language. We are subjects within the "prison house" of language.

From the Marxist perspective of language and ideology, however, that "prison house" doesn't completely

Mikhail Bakhtin

confine us. First of all, the concept of interpellation into an ideology—the subject's recognition of itself in the ideology's "hey you!" hailing—also allows for the rejection of that interpellation, the refusal of the subject to recognize itself as being addressed by the "you." The possibility of not responding to an ideological calling creates a "bad subject"—one who neither acts on, nor believes in, a particular ideological subject positioning.

In his essay "Discourse in the Novel" (1934-1935), the Russian literary theorist Mikhail Bakhtin shifts the thinking from "language" as a unitary (and restrictive) structure to "languages" as socially embedded forms of speech. He calls these languages "social speech types," or sociolects, and he's particularly interested in how these sociolects function within the specific form of the novel.

According to Bakhtin, a single "national" language contains multiple stratifications: the languages of professional groups, of generations, of regions, of enthusiasts (Go Broncos!), of authorities, etc., etc. He emphasizes the multiplicity of such languages and their continual evolution through usage: "Each day has its own slogan, its own vocabulary, its own emphases."

These languages, or sociolects, also carry distinct forms of social power. Think of the languages of doctors, lawyers, and professors as disciplinary languages. They are not just different vocabularies. They are specific forms for manifesting intentions and beliefs, for making conceptualizations concrete. This follows from Althusser's idea that there is no belief without practice, and no practice without belief. Bakhtin points out that every language choice you make in the course of a day is a practice, making visible/verbal your (conscious or unconscious) ideological positioning in any given situation.

"Language" is only unitary, Bakhtin argues, in abstract, grammatical normative forms. The idea of one *correct* way of speaking/writing ignores all the *other* ways real people talk. "All living languages," says Bakhtin, are always in an "uninterrupted process of historical becoming" that cannot be confined to the rules of grammar. Languages for Bakhtin are alive and changing and doing things in the world, rather than just existing as structures. He brings us back to the idea that "we speak language," rather than being entirely constructed by it.

We speak an enormous variety of sociolects, of ideological languages, in the course of a day. Bakhtin calls all these languages HETEROGLOSSIA—a multiplicity of ways of speaking that reflect and create social relationships and forms of social power.

A Classroom Dramatization

The Cast: six volunteers, in three pairs

The Scenario: There has been a Halloween party out of control; a window is broken, a laptop ruined.

Act One: partygoer speaking to best friend, explaining how it happened

Act Two: partygoer speaking to parents, explaining how it happened

Act Three: partygoer speaking to police, explaining how it happened

What this play is about: three different social situations, three different power dynamics, three different "languages."

Bakhtin points out that no sociolect, no "language" or social speech type, exists entirely on its own. Every language that exists in a particular culture at a particular time has a history, and the words from earlier eras coexist with current words. Similarly, while every age group and every family has its own language, the words in those languages also belong to other languages, in which they have different meanings. The word "sick" means something different when spoken between college students than when spoken between a doctor and patient! Words in any sociolect are always already socially embedded in other sociolects; words "belong" to particular ways of thinking, particular ideologies.

All languages, Bakhtin maintains, are "specific points of view on the world, forms for conceptualizing the world in words." Languages, he says, "encounter one another and coexist in the consciousness of real people." There are no "neutral" words or forms, words that belong to no one; every word used by a conscious being is an ideological choice. As Bakhtin put it, "For any individual consciousness living in it, language is not an abstract system of normative forms but a concrete heteroglot conception of the world."

Each word used by a subject tastes of all the contexts in which it has lived its socially charged life. Every word pre-exists an individual, but the individual infuses each word with a new intention, a new meaning. An individual or group can REACCENTUATE a word or sign, giving it new meaning. A classic example is the "N-word": used as a racist epithet it means one thing, used in rap music it means something else.

Words accumulate meaning as they are used. Every word always carries a history of its use and meaning, but it can always be made to mean more than that. For Bakhtin, language is not a prison house of predefined terms, but a living activity that has a history and is always in the process of becoming. We as language users can create, re-

accentuate, redefine, and remake our languages. In doing so, we acknowledge our words as social entities that convey intentions, beliefs, and actions.

For Bakhtin, as for most Marxist theorists, language is always a material practice. He would reject the structuralist conception of language as an empty, abstract set of grammatical rules. Instead he sees language as a living, evolving *process*, always embodied in the act of speaking. For Bakhtin, this means you can never separate language from language usage: words have meaning because they do things in the real social world. Using language always happens by and through subjects, just like Althusser's conception of "ideology."

Bakhtin emphasizes the social nature of language in order to identify two primary modes of speaking: the **monologic** and the **dialogic**. As you know, a "dialogue" is a conversation between two people (or more). But Bakhtin adds an essential third element to the formula: the social relationship between the two speakers. When all three elements are present, the operations of language move between the speakers according to each speaker's perception of the social relationship being enacted.

In contrast to the dialogic mode, monologic speech is language that comes from a single speaker. A monologue doesn't allow for any kind of interaction between speakers; it is a univocal use of language—only one voice speaking. Monologic speech is directed at an audience that does not talk back. The social relationship created in a monologue is like that of professor and student: the person with the power does the talking, the powerless do the listening.

Bakhtin uses this distinction, or binary opposition, to examine literary forms. Poetry, he maintains, is monologic, while novels—narrative fiction—is always dialogic.

Let's unpack that. According to Bakhtin, literary criticism, or literary evaluation, has always created and maintained a binary opposition: poetry/fiction. In this pair, he points out, poetry is the favored term and fiction is the subordinated term. Poetry has always gotten more attention than novels; verse is posited as the "higher" or more important literary form. The reason, he says, is that existing modes of literary analysis have been primarily interested in "stylistics"—reading a poem to reveal what is "poetic" about the way it presents language. He is thinking mostly about formalism and New Criticism, which limited literary analysis to "the words on the page" without regard for anything exterior to the text. This mode of "close reading" works beautifully with poetry, not so well for novels.

Thus, Bakhtin writes, all criticism and theory is "oriented toward the single-languaged and single-styled genres." Formalist critics look at language usage as disconnected from any kind of social relations; they separate the literary work from any of its social engagements (via author or audience) and thereby elevate the poem to the highest level of literary art.

Poetry is thus monologic. A formalist critic reads the poem as if it comes from a single unitary voice or source, and refers to nothing except itself. A poem is read "as if it were a hermetic and self-sufficient whole, whose elements constitute a closed system presuming nothing beyond themselves." Poetry is language that is self-referential rather than socially situated.

And so, according to Mikhail Bakhtin, the formalist reads the poetic word as "autotelic": something that refers only to itself and not to a real external social world with real human speakers trying to DO something with their speech. Think of it this way: poetry is like a piece of art you hang on the wall—it's pretty but it doesn't do anything. A novel is more like a dishwasher—it does things, performs functions, in the real everyday world. Poems use language without social reality or actual speakers; novels present us with lots of people, lots of speech, and lots of social interactions.

143

The critical prejudice in favor of poetry as more "literary" or more "aesthetic" than prose labels novels as something unworthy of critical attention. But Bakhtin objects to this: "[T]he categories and methods of traditional stylistics remain incapable of dealing effectively with the artistic uniqueness of discourse in the novel," he writes.

To think about how novels use language differently than poetry does, Bakhtin suggests that we go back to the ancient Greeks, who divided language study into two fields: poetics and rhetoric. Although literary criticism has followed the trajectory of the *Poetics* of Aristotle and his followers, it has ignored Aristotle's *Rhetoric*. Bakhtin proposes that literary critical study of the novel as a literary form must begin with the novel's roots in classical rhetoric, not poetics.

So what is this "rhetoric" that forms the basis for the novel?

Rhetoric is the art of discourse. Studying rhetoric means studying the ways writers and speakers employ words to inform, persuade, or motivate particular audiences in specific situations. We encounter rhetoric in political speeches, where candidates try to use language that will persuade you to vote for them. Rhetoric is finding the appropriate language—an appropriate "sociolect"—that unites the speaker and the audience, and effectively conveys the ideas that the speaker wants the audience to get. Thus, rhetoric is fundamentally about social relationships and socially embedded language; it is a way to see language at work, not just sitting on a page.

Rhetoric is closely associated with argument, and therefore with ideological beliefs and actions. Aristotle divided rhetoric into three main styles or modes of persuasion: **logos, pathos, and ethos**. Logos was an appeal to logic and reason, pathos an appeal to empathy and affect, and ethos an appeal to moral and legal sensibilities. Rhetoric is one of the three ancient arts of discourse, along with grammar and logic. Together rhetoric, grammar, and logic are called "the Trivium" (from which we get the word "trivia").

Bakhtin argues that reading the novel from the tradition of rhetoric means moving away from looking at language as a formal impersonal structure detached from actual usage, and moving toward a view of language as a living, breathing, changing mode of human expression, persuasion, and argument. Novels then can be seen as fundamentally dialogic, while poetry is fundamentally monologic.

The novel is dialogic because it is heteroglossic; it is built from a variety of sociolects or languages as used by the characters in their interactions. A novel may include the language of romance, of legal struggle, of journalism, of economics, of religion, of politics. Moreover, each of these languages is situated and used in some "real world" setting—as if the characters were, like us, speaking in specific social situations for specific purposes.

Within a dialogic model, every utterance is oriented toward the "conceptual horizon" of the audience. A speaker chooses what to say, what language to use, in order to connect with the internal languages the listener already knows. Dialogic speech and rhetoric are ways of using language that work to maximize the overlap between the sociolects of the speaker and those of the respondent. This is why Bakhtin says that our words always belong both to us and to someone else; they are in our mouths and others' mouths. As he puts it, "Discourse lives on the boundary between its own context and another, alien context."

More Foucault

Foucault is FOUCAULT the way Freud is FREUD and Marx is MARX—the named founder of a sweeping worldview, a revolutionary mode of analysis and understanding. Or what Foucault himself calls an "episteme."

An episteme is a way of thinking that creates order and meaning according to some kind of logic. In his book *The Order of Things: An Archaeology of the Human Sciences* (1966), Foucault uses an image from a story by Jorge Luis Borges to illustrate the idea of a logical classification system:

[I]n a certain Chinese Encyclopedia, the Celestial Emporium of Benevolent Knowledge, it is written that animals are divided into:

    1. those that belong to the Emperor,

    2. embalmed ones,

    3. those that are trained,

    4. suckling pigs,

    5. mermaids,

    6. fabulous ones,

    7. stray dogs,

    8. those included in the present classification,

    9. those that tremble as if they were mad,

    10. innumerable ones,

    11. those drawn with a very fine camelhair brush,

    12. others,

    13. those that have just broken a flower vase,

    14. those that from a long way off look like flies.

Ridiculous, right? But how is that classification system any different from the one used in Western science—the "Kingdom, Phylum, Class, Order, Family, Genus, Species"

method of classifying life? Both do the same thing: organize information to create knowledge.

How does our culture organize knowledge? One of the primary systems by which Western culture creates, archives, and transmits authoritative knowledge is the university. I think of the structure at the University of Colorado, where I work, as fairly typical. The university is divided into schools and colleges, which in turn are divided into "disciplines" or departments. Each discipline has its own objects of inquiry (the stuff it thinks about), and each has its own methods, assumptions, preconceptions, paradigms, worldviews, and ideologies (how it thinks about the stuff it thinks about). Each discipline also has its own language, in Bakhtin's sense, and each discipline produces "discourse" in that language in the form of published research.

But wait. "Discipline" has two meanings. It's a field of thought or inquiry, but it's also a method of ensuring or correcting behavior. Foucault's works explore what these two meanings have in common, through his concept of...

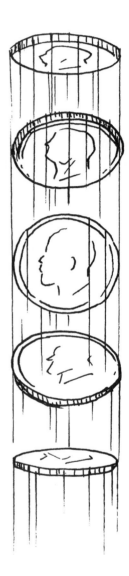

Power/Knowledge

But this one is NOT a binary opposition. Foucault says that power and knowledge are inextricably linked, two sides of the same coin. He's rewriting the cliché "knowledge is power." The "knowledge" part of Foucault's "power/knowledge" consists of all the things produced within

university disciplines. Think of the phrase "studies have shown that...." The idea is that there is some expert, or group of experts, who have examined a question according to their discipline and drawn conclusions that then can be put into practice. My discipline is called "English," and "literature" is the object around which my discipline produces knowledge.

OK, so what's the "power" part of "power/knowledge" within the discipline of literary studies? Foucault points us toward the intersection of "author" and "authority," where the production of discourse (writing) requires accountability and attribution.

In pre-modern European cultures, the reliability of knowledge depended on the author's reputation; naming the author was the equivalent of proving the authority of your source: "Aristotle said..." "St. Paul said..."

The author's name serves a whole set of social functions, according to Foucault. But, he points out, not every piece

of writing has an "author": a private letter has a signatory, a contract has an underwriter, and an anonymous poster (or graffiti) has a writer but not an author. "The function of the author," says Foucault, "is to characterize the existence, circulation, and operation of certain discourses within a society."

What makes a text need an author? Why do some types of writing need or deserve authorship?

Foucault says that a text requires an author because the circulation of some ideas requires a name to be attached to them in order to CONTROL the ideas: "Speeches and books were assigned real authors ... only when the author became subject to punishment ... to the extent that his discourse was considered transgressive."

This mode of authority, Foucault points out, was gradually replaced by the authority of scientific discourse, which relies on the reproducibility of results rather than on

the name of a specific author or scientist. The specific subject disappeared from scientific discourse, except for names that demarcate a theoretical shift (Newton's physics, for example). Science has authority precisely because it is a subjectless discourse, not dependent on any one author.

In modern Western culture, scientific discourse has authority; science tells us the truth about the world. Foucault's works investigate how scientific knowledges are deployed as forms of power. He specifically focuses on how knowledges produced in the "human sciences"—sociology, psychology, medicine, psychiatry—have informed public policy and governmental practices about mental illness, criminality, and sexual "deviance."

Foucault is particularly interested in **biopower**: "the set of mechanisms through which the basic biological features of the human species become the object of a political strategy, of a general strategy of power." According to Foucault, the industrial capitalist nation-state, emerging in the late 18th century, created technologies of biopower deployed to make subjects into efficient and productive workers. Institutions like Althusser's ISAs taught people to be "normal," self-regulating subjects who know and obey the laws.

Foucault's work focuses more on the technologies created for "bad subjects," those whose self-regulation needs discipline and correction. In his book *Discipline and Punish: The Birth of the Prison* (1975), Foucault points to the 18th-century British reformer Jeremy Bentham as the architect of new technologies that created order and regulation through discipline and surveillance. Bentham designed a new kind of prison, called the Panopticon, that consisted

of a central tower surrounded by a ring of individual cells. Authorities in the tower could see into every cell, but the inmates could not see into the tower to know if they were being watched. The constant surveillance—or the constant *possibility* of surveillance—was enough to guarantee good behavior for the majority of prisoners, and transgressors could be easily seen.

The Eye of Mordor! A model for the surveillance state: subjects behave because *somebody* is always watching.

Chapter 7
RACE AND POSTCOLONIALISM

"Race," like gender, can be defined as a set of cultural signs assigned by various social mechanisms to human bodies. The physical traits of these bodies become signifiers of race. "Racism" is reading the signifiers of race—eye shape, skin color, hair texture—as pointing to some stable (and often derogatory) signifieds, concepts about what skin color *means.*

When I say "race," I'm using a 19th-century definition of the term. Here "race" is an identity structure in the physiological distinction among various ethnicities and cultural groups. In that sense, perhaps, we are in (or nearing) a post-racial culture: the biological markers, or physical

Toni Morrison

traits, that were used in the 19th and 20th centuries to designate a method of classification known as "race" are less important today in creating ideologies of race than are all the associations that have accrued to a racial category. Toni Morrison says it best:

> Race has become metaphorical—a way of referring to and disguising forces, events, classes, and expressions of social decay and

155

economic division far more threatening to the body politic than biological "race" ever was.

In this regard, race is everywhere. Even things that are not "about" race are always about race.

Where "race" exists as sign and metaphor, racism is the systematic empowerment of certain signifiers and the disempowerment of others. Looking at racism from Foucault's perspective, we would look for the forms of power/knowledge that support and perpetuate the ideologies and practices that read signifiers of difference as signifiers of inequality.

Henry Louis Gates, Jr.

Harvard historian (and television journalist) Henry Louis Gates, Jr., is one of the leading figures in African American literary theory. In his 1983 essay "The Blackness of Black-

ness: A Critique of the Sign on the Signifying Monkey," Gates explores how questions of race affect strategies of interpretation. When we in literary studies read African American literature, what kind of critical, interpretive, or theoretical frameworks do we use?

Gates looks at the rhetorical

Henry Louis Gates, Jr.   traditions, coming from the Greeks,

in which Western cultures have formulated their modes of writing, argument, and analysis. He follows the (white) literary critic Harold Bloom in naming the major tropes, or forms of figurative language, that are central to the Western tradition of rhetoric.

What's a trope? **Trope** is a general word for any kind of figurative (as opposed to literal) language. Its meaning in Greek is "to turn," as in "to turn a phrase." Using a trope "turns" the argument or discussion toward a nonliteral use of language.

The major tropes as identified by Bloom are: metaphor, metonymy, synecdoche, irony, hyperbole, litotes, and metalepsis. Gates, however, points out in his article that all of these tropes—all of these ways of creating and using figurative language—come from the Greek tradition in Western culture. Kenneth Burke, another white literary critic, called them "the master tropes"; Gates calls them "the master's tropes."

Gates wants to look instead to African cultural traditions—to African myths and their forms of figurative language—to formulate ways to read African American texts. He argues that, in order to understand the ways that African American cultures and writers use figurative or rhetorical language, we need to look to African civilizations rather than European ones.

According to Gates, African American cultures have their own forms of trope: marking, loud-talking, testifying, calling out, rapping, playing the dozens. In some of these, participants engage with each other through rituals of insult and put-down. The contestants "win" if they keep their cool and come up with ever more clever insults (rather than physical violence as retaliation). The dozens, a kind of rapping, is a game of power language.

Gates groups these practices under the general heading of SIGNIFYING. He's playing, obviously, with Saussure's idea of signifying and signification. (He's troping on Saussure.) Signfying—or **signifyin'**—has a different meaning and practice in African American communities, one that Gates traces back to African cultural myths and traditions.

Specifically, Gates looks at a figure in Yoruba mythology called "the signifying monkey," also known as Esu. The signifying monkey is a trickster figure (like coyote or raven in Native American mythology) that acts as a mediator between warring factions within a culture, using wit, humor, and mischief to defuse conflicts.

Gates's article spends a lot of time tracing the movement of the myth of the signifying monkey from the Yoruba culture of Nigeria and Benin through the routes of slavery. He sees in this myth an "unbroken arc of metaphysical presuppositions and patterns of figuration shared through space and time among black cultures in West Africa, South

America, the Caribbean, and the United States."

The Signifying Monkey, in all its diasporic appearances in African-based cultures, is a messenger between the gods and people. He is guardian of the crossroads, a master of style and the stylus, a phallic god of generation, and the master of the barrier between earth and the divine realm.

Sound familiar? Esu is the Yoruba equivalent of the Greek god Hermes—or the other way around: Hermes is the Western version of Esu. Hermes is also the god of secrets and codes, from which we get the word **hermeneutics**, or interpretation. English majors like to look at literary texts from a hermeneutical perspective, reading to interpret or decode.

So Gates looks at Esu to formulate an "Esu-neutics:" a metaphor for the act of interpretation "for the critic of comparative black literature." Interpretation, in this Africanist mythology, is "to unite or unknot knowledge" or "to turn or translate." The Yoruba version of our "close reading" is called "reading the signs." Gates points out that Esu is "the black interpreter," the Yoruba god of **indeterminacy**.

Gates links Esu with the contemporary African American

practice of signifyin'. This refers to "the trickster's ability to talk with great innuendo, to carp, cajole, needle, and lie ... to talk around a subject ... to make fun of a person or situation ... speaking with the hands and eyes," especially to stir or trouble or mock an authority figure. Signifyin' is "a technique of indirect argument or persuasion," "to imply, goad, beg, boast" or insult.

Signifyin' is what you are doing when you tell a "yo mama" joke:

> *Yo mama is so fat, when she wears a yellow raincoat, people yell "Taxi!"*

> *Yo mama is so stupid, I told her Christmas was right around the corner—so she went looking for it.*

> *Yo mama so stupid she tried to put her M&Ms in alphabetical order.*

Yo Mama jokes are ritual insults that generate more insults (rather than violence). They are a form of linguistic play that works to recirculate cultural power between members of a subordinated group.

Gates's essay goes on to discuss Zora Neale Hurston's definition of signifyin' in her 1937 novel *Their Eyes Were*

Watching God as a vehicle for an oppressed women's liberation and a rhetorical strategy in the narration of fiction.

Gates assumes that you know African American literary traditions and histories. He makes reference (without explanation) to Hurston, Ralph Ellison, Ishmael Reed, Jean Toomer, W.E.B. Du Bois, Toni Morrison, Sterling Brown, Alice Walker, and Richard Wright. He argues that black writers read and critique other black writers' texts as acts of rhetorical self-definition. We could also call this **intertextuality**—black authors in conversation with each other and with those who have come before. Gates argues that these conversations make African American literature fundamentally dialogic—literary texts troping on the tropes used in prior literary texts.

And so, Gates argues, through the critical framework of African trickster traditions of signifyin', one can better understand the way African American writers are signifyin' not only within their texts but also *between* their texts— Ralph Ellison signifyin' on Richard Wright, Ishmael Reed signifyin' on Wright and Ellison, and so on. Gates compares this to the riffing in improvisational jazz, where one instrument picks up the line from the previous one and "tropes" it.

All of this, he says, is a mode of understanding how language and rhetoric operate within formations of power/ knowledge, either to reinforce existing structures of power or to disrupt them. The rhetorical strategies of subordinated groups, of disenfranchised or disempowered groups, work like the Signifying Monkey to undermine the authority of the dominant culture and to empower the subordinated—all by the power of language.

Trinh T. Minh-Ha and Gloria Anzaldúa

Can you tell, by my writing, that I am white? Is writing always racially marked?

Whiteness exists, in American culture, as the "unmarked" category, the nonracial category. Whiteness is taken as the norm, the default position, and generally race is only specified when it's non-white. In the dominant culture, whiteness = selfhood, and non-whiteness = otherness. How, then, can non-white, non-selves have any sense of "I"dentity?

Trinh T. Minh-Ha

According to the Vietnamese filmmaker and literary theorist Trinh T. Minh-ha, "identity ... has long been a notion that relies on the concept of an essential, authentic core that remains hidden to one's consciousness and that requires the elimination of all that is considered foreign or not true to the self, that is to say, not-I, other."

162

In other words, what makes you who you are is primarily that there is a "not-you" out there; each self is defined by having a not-self, an other who enables one to occupy the "self" position. This way of thinking should be fairly familiar by this point in our study of literary theory; it draws on the same logic as Saussure's negative relations of value and Derrida's binary oppositions.

Thus, the concept self or identity is held in place, or stabilized, by being paired with its binary opposite, the other. Being a self requires establishing a boundary between self and other, and maintaining/enforcing that boundary at all costs. This sets up a dynamic whereby Subject A is invested in having a stable identity and achieves that (in part) by casting itself as not-B. Subject A then wants B to be not-A consistently and constantly. B thus achieves a stable position (in relation to A, and in terms set by A), though that position is not recognized as "self" or "subject" in the same way that A's has been recognized. A then needs some form of power to keep B in the position it desires B to stay in. A uses that power to dictate the terms in which B can make claims to identity or selfhood.

The obvious problem, as Trinh and other theorists point out, is that B never gets to become a self, since A always keeps B in the position of other; B's place and social function is always relative to A's selfhood. But this is also a problem for A, who is just as structured by this binary opposition as B is.

Trinh wants to find some other way to theorize identity than through the binary self/other opposition. She wants to find new ways to think about difference, so that "difference" doesn't form a binary opposite to "sameness." If difference, or "otherness," doesn't define the possibilities for "sameness," or identity, then we can come up with new ways of thinking about the relations between sameness and difference, selfhood and otherness.

Finally, Trinh talks about another way to rethink concepts of identity so that they don't rely on the self/other dichotomy. She invokes the idea of the "inappropriate oth-

er"—the "other" who refuses the position of otherness and insists on speaking and acting as subject, despite the efforts of (usually Western) "selves" to define them as "other." An inappropriate other acts out, refuses to behave correctly, and thereby also becomes an "inappropriated other"—a subject whose being cannot be appropriated by another to serve another's purposes. An inappropriate(d) other has agency, is capable of resisting appropriation and of recognizing and negotiating her situations, including her own subjectivity/identity.

This is one of the major themes that Gloria Anzaldúa brings up. As a queer Chicana, she highlights her differences from both the dominant Anglo American culture and her own family, her *raza,* her culture. In any context, she is other. She refuses this otherness, however, and situates herself as an "untamed tongue"—an inappropriated other who writes her own map of subjectivity and selfhood.

The metaphor of a map is useful here, as the title of Anzaldúa's best-known book—the semi-autobiographical *Borderlands/La Frontera* (1983)—invokes the idea of boundaries between countries and between cultures. As a queer Chicana, she places herself in a borderland: a

Gloria Anzaldúa

place that is defined by otherness but that is between categories and countries.

What is the border? It is a marginalized, liminal space of contradictions, a space of shifting multiple identities. Life on the border is life in the shadow. The border is where two or more cultures, classes, races, or ideologies edge or confront each other. There is a space between cultures, classes, races, sexual orientations—call them worlds or worldviews—where they meld and mix, where they are both worlds/worldviews and neither worlds/worldviews. These are what Anzaldúa calls *los intersticios*—the interstices, or spaces between.

Anzaldúa's essay explores three categories of alienation, or the three ways in which she experiences her own otherness to her homeland: her gender and sexual identity, as queer; her linguistic identity, as a speaker of multiple sociolects/dialects; and her racial/cultural identity.

Let's start with that. Anzaldúa was born in 1942 to a migrant worker family in Texas. Thus, she was American by birth and Hispanic by racial classification. Specifically, she identified as "Tejano," or an Hispanic person living in Texas. But she also identified as mestiza, meaning she is of both Hispanic and Indian/indigenous origins. All in all, her racial identity contradicts the neat either/or boxes on the US census forms.

In a section of her book called "Half and Half," Anzaldúa talks about another set of borders or boundaries: those that govern gender and sexual identity. She tells of a woman who

was female for six months of
the year and male for the other six months: the woman is
mita y mita, or "half and half."
As a lesbian, Anzaldúa, claims
identity with both sexes: "I,
like other queer people, am
two in one body, both male
and female," limited only by
the "despot duality that says
we are able to be only one or
the other."

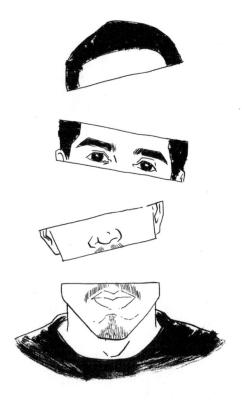

Anzaldúa's lesbian iden-
tity is part of her marginal-
ization, or "border" status,
within her own Chicana Cath-
olic culture. She points out that there are only three accept-
able roles for women in the migrant labor culture: wife and
mother, prostitute, and nun. Anzaldúa, who started men-
struating when she was only three because of an endocrine
imbalance, was already labeled "other" than normally female. Her queerness forced her away from the three standard female options and into a fourth: education and escape. This required her to break from the paradigms of her
family of origin and her cultures of origin, and to "forge her
own territory."

But this escape meant alienation from her people, from
La Raza, from her roots and origins. She discusses this in

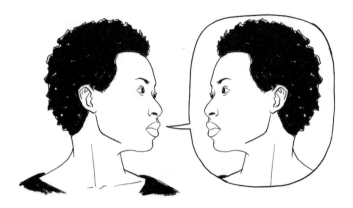

the section of her book called "Homophobia," where she realizes that homophobia is a "fear of going home"—of being turned away at the border of one's homeland, by one's motherland.

Her racial identity as mestiza and her sexual identity as queer make Anzaldúa "other"; they destabilize the convenient binaries of race and sexuality upheld as "normal." Even more importantly, her multiple identities are reflected in and created by the languages she speaks.

Anzaldúa says that our languages speak us; they define our identity, our cultural makeup, our ideologies, our definition of self. "Language is a homeland," she writes. *"Un lenguaje que corresponde a un modo de vivir."* And, she goes on, "ethnic identity is twin skin to linguistic identity—I am my language."

Anzaldúa identifies herself as a speaker of eight different languages, or sociolects:

    1) standard English

    2) working-class English

3) standard Spanish

4) standard Mexican Spanish

5) north Mexican Spanish dialect

6) Chicano Spanish

7) Tex-Mex

8) pachuco

Each of these languages can be "other" to the others: if she speaks Tex-Mex, she is not speaking standard English or standard Spanish. Whatever language she chooses, she will mark herself as alien to some cultures to which she belongs.

Where does she "belong"? Where is home for someone who speaks eight dialects? Which is her native, mother tongue?

Perhaps none. Could there be a "border" language? People who live in the borderland are *"deslenguadas,"* she writes. *"Somos los del español deficiente.* We are your linguistic nightmare, your linguistic aberration, your linguistic *mestizaje,* the subject of your *burla.* Because we speak with tongues of fire we are culturally crucified. Racially, culturally, and linguistically *somos huerfanos*—we speak an orphan tongue."

Edward Said and Postcolonialism

I am an English professor. What does that mean?

"English" denotes a nationality. And a language. And a field of study. What do all of these have to do with each other?

169

Let's take the question back to Foucault and the idea that the university produces knowledges, via discourse, that inform practices. How does power/knowledge work in the discourse of literary studies, in an English department?

Edward W. Said

"English" for me defines a field of study—literature in English—which carries with it sets of ideological beliefs and practices. In brief, the field we call "English" is defined through ideas about nationality: the entity we call "England" demarcates the boundaries of what we study in the English department. But those ideas of nationality designate more than just a geographical boundary. What is "English" is what has been claimed by England as belonging to English culture. There is thus a history and a politics connected with the idea of "English" as an area of cultural study.

Let's think about history first. From the late 17th century through the middle of the 20th century, England (as part of Great Britain) extended its national rule to countries and regions all over the world: to North America, to Africa, to the Islamic world of the Middle East, to India, East Asia, the West Indies, South America, and Polynesia. In doing so, it created colonies in these lands and, in most cases, took over the administration of government. Its laws and customs ruled people who lived half a world away from the country

"England."

British colonial rule (and all other Western nations who formed colonies, such as France and Germany) depended on a view of the indigenous populations of the colonized areas as inferior—that these populations needed the "advanced civilization" offered by Western culture. In fact, as the Palestinian-born scholar Edward Said argued, the West (or Occident) *produced* the discourses that described the non-white, non-Western cultures and peoples as inferior.

One of the impetuses for colonization was, of course, the spread of capitalism. Colonies provided sources of raw materials, cheap labor, and new markets for Western goods. But while the history of colonialism is very much caught up in the economics of capitalism, colonialism was by no mean confined to the economic realm. When an imperial power like Great Britain colonized a non-Western region, it exported its legal, religious, educational, military, political, and aesthetic ideas along with its economic system (what Marx would call the superstructure and Althusser would call the Ideological State Apparatus). In places like Africa and India, British colonial rule meant teaching the indigenous people about the superiority of Western ideals and institution—by

setting up systems of law and law enforcement following the British system; by sending missionaries to convert natives to Christianity (chiefly Anglicanism, or the Church of England) and establishing churches and seminaries; and by setting up schools to teach British customs, British history, and the English language to children and adults. And with these ideological exportations came British/ Western "culture" in the form of music, art, and literature— so that, regardless of the ancient literary traditions of India and the Arab world, inhabitants of these colonized areas were taught that Chaucer, Shakespeare, and Milton were the "greatest" authors in history. In short, British cultural standards were upheld and all other notions of cultural expression were denounced as inferior and subordinated to Western standards.

And this is part of what the academic "English" department was originally designed to do—study and assert the mastery of English language and literature as expressions of the most important and advanced civilization ever known. English departments were part of the process of establishing the hegemony (dominance) of English culture worldwide.

Postcolonial literary theory takes on the politics of the study of "English" literature and culture from the perspective of those who were colonized by it. Postcolonial theory questions whether an English department must necessarily reinforce the hegemony of Western cultural practices and thus support the political and economic forces that have subordinated what we have come to call the "Third World."

Said's book *Orientalism* (1978), and the writings of most postcolonial theorists, address how this happens. How is it that a colonized people come to accept that the ways of the colonizer are "better" than their own ways of organizing their culture?

Said uses the term "Orientalism" to refer to the set of discursive practices—i.e., the forms of power/knowledge— that Western Anglo-European cultures have used to produce and control the area of the globe they call "the Orient." The stereotypes associated with the words "Orient" and "Oriental" label that region as a place of mystery and exoticism. Such "otherness" exists only in relation to the familiarity of the Western Anglo-European world; the basis of Orientalism, like the basis of any form of racism or ethnocentrism, is the idea that "we" are the "selves" who are "familiar" and that "others" are necessarily "exotic."

"The Orient" is the right side of a binary opposition; the other side is "The Occident." The terms mean "east" and "west," respectively—but from whose perspective? What is "the Orient" east of?

The answer, of course, is that the Orient is east from the Anglo-European perspective. The concept of the Orient, and the very ideas of Eastern and Western cultures, are a product of the ways that Anglo-European explorers drew the map of the world from the 17th century onward. Said's book quotes the Italian cultural philosopher Giambattista Vico, who said that "men must take seriously that what they know is what they have made, and extend it to geography." Said expands on this idea, saying that "it is the map that engenders the territory" and not the territory that engenders the map. In other words, maps are not just representations of a "real world" that is out there, a way to locate where rivers and mountains are. Rather, *maps are texts,* like literary texts, that carry with them a cultural perspective, a way of constructing "reality" with an ideological basis.

An example of this is how the world figures time. In international time, there is a 24-hour clock, and the Earth is divided into 24 time zones. Where does time begin? In Greenwich, England. 0:00 is midnight GMT (Greenwich

Mean Time), and the rest of the world measures time in relation to GMT. The same idea works with longitude: zero degrees longitude, the "starting point" of global navigation, runs just east of London.

In both of these examples, England is the center of the world, the place where time and space begin, the starting point for all other models of mapping. That's because England drew the maps and created the time-measuring system. And that's because England was the largest colonial power in the modern world and had the power to "create" the knowledge of the entire globe.

The history of imperialism is the history of discourse about colonized places, whether in the form of official government reports, personal travel narratives, or imaginative fiction set in "exotic" foreign lands. You might think of Joseph Conrad's 1899 novella *The Heart of Darkness* as an example of imperial discourse—a work of literature that shows the contradictions and collapse of imperial forms of power/knowledge. Said argues that the creation of discourse about a colonized culture, about "the other," works also to silence that colonized culture, which cannot "talk back." Rather, such discourse renders the people of the colonized culture as powerless subjects of Western power/ knowledge. Anything the colonized culture tries to say or write about itself is by definition considered illegitimate, non-knowledge, nonsense.

Postcolonial literary studies, and postcolonial theory in general, focus on what happens when the formerly colonized culture starts to, or insists on, producing its own knowledge about itself. What happens when "the empire writes back" to the dominant culture, when the silenced subjects of knowledge insist on becoming the producers of knowledge?

One way to think about this is through the lens of deconstruction. The discourses that establish the colonizers as knowers and the colonized as subjects of knowledge all depend on our old friend, the structure of binary oppositions—in this case, West/East, Occident/ Orient, civilized/native, self/other, educated/ignorant. When "the empire writes back," these binary oppositions are deconstructed. When a colonized subject insists on taking up the position of "self"—the creator of knowledge about his/her own culture rather than the subject of that knowledge—these binary oppositions start to fall apart.

Postcolonial theorists and scholars argue a lot about the meaning of the word "postcolonial," particularly about when a "postcolonial" theory or literature begins to emerge. In this book, we'll stick with the easy definition: "postcolonial" designates the time after colonial rule, mostly in the mid- to late-20th century. This was the era when most of the British colonies, such as India, fought for their independence and became separate, sovereign nations. Postcolonial theories began to arise in the 1960s, as thinkers from the former colonies began to create their own forms of knowledge, their own discourses, to counter the discourses of colonialism. These postcolonial discourses articulated the experience of the colonized rather than the colonizer, giving what's called the "subaltern"—the subordinated non-white, non-Western subject of colonial rule—a voice.

Homi Bhabha

Colonizers used Foucauldian mechanisms of discipline and punishment to get the colonized to be "like us"—native peoples were subject to colonial laws and required to be obedient to the colonizers. Colonizers also used all of the ideological apparatuses that Althusser discussed, building Western churches, schools, clubs, and organizations that would create the proper Western self-regulating subjects, who had learned and internalized the colonizer's values and worldviews. If successful, such reshaping of the "savage" would not only eliminate "savagery," but would also instill in the colonized a desire to become Western subjects and

Homi Bhabha

177

to *welcome* the takeover. The colonizer's ideal was to make the savage like "us," to identify with "us," and to make them friendly, respectful, and obedient to "us."

How did that work for the savages and the selves, the colonized and the colonizers? Homi Bhabha, an Indian-born postcolonial theorist, argues that the need to maintain the binary structures of Western thought, to preserve the self/other opposition, made it impossible for a colonized subject to cross the slash and become a "self." The colonizer had the power to decide who was a self and who wasn't, and the colonial gaze always required the presence of an other. So even the indigenous people who adopted Western perspectives and ideologies, who acted like colonizers, could never become full subjects on the same footing with the colonizers.

Here is the concept of the "subaltern" as developed by Gayatri Spivak, another Indian American postcolonialist: the native who buys into the colonizer's ideologies and does what s/he is told to do by the colonizers in order to become a self/citizen/civilized, yet is never recognized as such by the colonizers. The subaltern is the colonized subject positioned within colonial power structures in order to achieve selfhood, but is never granted full selfhood or subjectivity by those power structures.

The subaltern is always a **hybrid** position, neither native nor colonial but a mixture of both. As a hybrid, the subaltern can be "like us" in the sense of a simile—they can be similar, but not identical, to the colonizer's "self." Bhabha points out that the subaltern's performance of Western selfhood is always a copy, a mimicry, even a parody, of that selfhood. By trying to be "like us" the subaltern is merely imitating, and perhaps mocking, "us."

This mimicry becomes a source of humor for the colonizers. *Ha ha! See how funny the natives look in Western clothes, trying to be civilized!* The 1956 film musical *The King and I,* for example, includes a comical scene in which the King's numerous concubines all wear hoop skirts and corsets but don't know how to move or sit in them.

From the colonizer's perspective, the subaltern's efforts to imitate civilized behavior are desirable and comic, but also potentially threatening: Are we laughing at them or are they laughing at us? If the subaltern is wearing a mask of "selfhood," then what's behind the mask? For the colonizer, there will always be something unknown and unknowable in the subaltern—the colonizer can never know if, beneath the performance of civilization, the savage still lurks. Bhabha points out that this fear often appears in colonial discourse as the "inscrutability" of the native—the part of the savage that can be covered up and hidden but never eliminated.

In his essay "Signs Taken for Wonders: Questions of Ambivalence and Authority" (1985), Bhabha asks what happens when a colonized people encounter an English book. Why is this important? Because the printed word, for most colonized populations, was unknown—mystical, magical, and thus a symbol of the greater wisdom and power of the colonizing culture.

To any culture in which information and ideologies are passed down via oral tradition—any culture the West would call "illiterate"—the idea that pieces of paper could "talk" was as astonishing as the wooden sticks that shot fire and killed. Both the book and the gun became symbols of colonial authority, helping to persuade the indigenous population to accept the colonizer's rules.

Bhabha's article describes various scenes in which a Western book appears in a non-Western colonized culture to emphasize the book's power as a symbol and metaphor of "civilization." Bhabha's description of natives in India who are reading a Bible is a much-repeated scenario in colonial discourse, especially reports written from colonizers back to the "mother country." (As Said argues, these become the *knowledge* the mother country has about the colony, and thus the basis for policies and practices that govern it.) Bhabha calls this scenario a foundational myth of Western culture: the moment when the native savage discovers the "miracle" of the English printed book.

The printed, bound book is also an indication of selfhood; if you can read it, you can be a Western self. But you have to read the book "correctly"—that is, as the colonizers read it.

A subaltern will always read the book incorrectly, according to Bhabha, because s/he can't read from the same context as the colonizer. When given colonial forms of subjectivity to inhabit, the subaltern can only simulate or parody them, perform them but not be them. The subaltern cannot inhabit the text of the book in the same way a colonizer does; hence the colonizer judges the subaltern's reading as wrong. The text, when read by the subaltern, becomes a nontext, a parody of a civilized reading; the subaltern can only misread and misinterpret the Western text.

Bhabha concludes that "the representation of colonial authority" in symbols of civilization like the English-language book "depends less on a universal symbol of English identity than on its productivity as a sign of difference." Reading the Bible may make you "like us," but you can't *read* like us, so you will always be misreading and misinterpreting—you will always be "other." The symbols of colonial power, like the book, continually produce differences between colonizer and colonized.

Chapter 8
POSTMODERNISM

According to the French literary theorist François Lyotard, in his book *The Postmodern Condition* (1984), the term "postmodern"

François Lyotard

> *designates the state of our culture following the transformations which, since the end of the nineteenth century, have altered the game rules for science, literature, and the arts.*

The "game rules" that he says have been altered are the rules that said language is capable of accurately representing the external world, capable of conveying meaning unequivocally and reliably.

Gilles Deleuze, another 20th-century Frenchman, writing about Friedrich Nietzsche, explains that the concept of "meaning" itself is problematic. A world of representation, full of signs, creates a framework of mystery that requires interpretation. A hermeneutic worldview affirms the idea that everything has a secret or hidden meaning that needs to be discovered. But, Deleuze argues, "the world" is just the operation of material forces in contention, without any inherent "meaning" or message for humans. The rational categories we use to order and understand the world are always only our creations, our own frameworks placed over the forces we observe and, by naming, think we master. We construct and understand our world in and through metaphors in order to give stability to the continual movement and flux of these material forces.

"All our thinking is fiction-making." —Nietzsche

According to Lyotard, postmodernism is an attitude of "incredulity toward metanarratives." A metanarrative, or "grand narrative," is the story an ideology tells itself— an ideology of ideologies. It's the "big picture" story that a mode of thinking, a theory, a worldview maintains in order to explain and legitimize its operations.

Take psychoanalysis, for example. The grand narrative of psychoanalysis is the tragedy of loss: psychoanalysis (whether Freudian or Lacanian) tells the story of an original, wonderful, primal unity, a world of fullness, flesh, and satisfaction that must be abandoned in order to become a civilized adult (properly heterosexual, properly

situated within a centered Symbolic linguistic system
that enables a subject to represent the world and the self
through the assumption of a connection between signifier
and signified—so that "I" has meaning). That original world
is irretrievably lost, but our longing for it continues forever
and remains a primary motivation for our acts and beliefs
and being.

Hmm, sound familiar? Adam and Eve and all that?
Psychoanalysis retells that grand narrative of human
existence—a worldview based on lack, absence, loss, and
guilt.

Lyotard contends that all aspects of modern society,
including science as the primary form of knowledge,
depend on such grand narratives. Postmodernism, then,
is the awareness that such narratives serve to mask the

contradictions and instabilities that are inherent in any social organization or practice. In rejecting grand narratives, postmodernism favors "mini-narratives"—stories that explain small practices or local events, rather than large-scale universal or global concepts. Postmodern mini-narratives are always situational, provisional, contingent, and temporary, making no claim to universality, truth, reason, or stability.

Postmodernism also critiques the Enlightenment idea that language is "rational," that language is a transparent medium through which to represent the real/perceivable world. This conception of language assumes that there is a signified behind every signifier, that language points to and names something "real" beyond itself, and that language *only* labels and points to, but does not alter or interfere with, what it names.

Modern societies depend on the idea that signifiers always point to signifieds, and that reality resides in signifieds. In a postmodern society, however, there are only signifiers, without signifieds. There is no stable "real" referent; there are only surfaces without depth.

According to postmodern theorist Jean Baudrillard (you guessed it, another Frenchman), our world consists of simulacra, copies or representations for which there is no original. Think of a "virtual reality" game that creates a total environment in which you dwell, unconscious of your real-world self and body. For Baudrillard, this is not a game but how the "real world" actually is. He points to Disneyland,

for example, as a simulacrum—a fantasy land that exists as representation, a world as "real" as TV or movies but that exists in three-dimensional material form. Mickey Mouse is, in this sense, more "real" than the president of the United States—for adults and for kids.

Postmodernism is also concerned with the organization of knowledge in contemporary global culture. Lyotard argues in *The Postmodern Condition* that modern societies have equated knowledge with science, with the grand

narratives of objectivity and legitimation. Science, then, stands in binary opposition to "narrative," the *other way* of knowing; narrative is the less valued, less rational, unscientific mode. If science produces truth, then narrative, in modern societies, produces fiction. If truth and science are aligned with other structuring binary oppositions, then narrative is identified with the primitive, irrational, female, mad, and disorderly.

Lyotard argues that science, like other modes of thought or worldviews, depends upon a grand narrative to explain its premises. What's important here is not the content of that grand narrative (you can probably tell the story yourself by now), but that science must posit its other, narrative, in order that it may be science—it must rely on that other to be itself. In other words, science needs narrative to be non-knowledge so that science can be knowledge, yet it relies on "non-knowledge," itself a grand narrative, to exist as knowledge.

Whether scientific or narrative, "knowledge" in modern societies has been upheld as good for its own sake: one gains knowledge, via education, to be "knowledgeable," to be an educated person. This is the ideal of a liberal arts education and a college curriculum based on the distribution of required courses across a variety of disciplines and fields. Such an education has been said to produce a well-rounded humanist for whom knowledge, in whatever form, is progress.

In a postmodern society, by contrast, the value of knowledge is said to lie in its usage, its function. If you major in any of the humanities, like literature or philosophy, you are certain to be asked "What will you *do* with your degree?" Increasingly, educational policies and institutions emphasize skills and training for employment rather than education "for its own sake." Knowledge is good only when it's put to use producing something.

Not only is knowledge in postmodern societies characterized by its utility, it is also distributed, stored, and arranged differently than in modern societies. Specifically, the advent of computer technologies has redefined "knowledge" as data, information that can be digitized; anything that can't be digitized will not be stored. The opposite of "knowledge," in postmodern societies, is not "ignorance" but "noise."

Deleuze and Guattari

In 1972, postmodern philosopher Gilles Deleuze teamed up with a Lacanian-trained former psychoanalyst

Gilles Deleuze

named Felix Guattari; together they wrote *Anti-Oedipus,* which formed the first volume in their series *Capitalism and Schizophrenia.*

Anti-Oedipus is (among many other things) a deconstruction of Freud's theory of the Oedipus complex that focuses on the psychoanalytic concept of "desire." For Freud, desire is libido, sexual drive, a primal unconscious force or instinct that has to be harnessed, sublimated, controlled, masked, renounced, hidden, or suppressed in order for a polymorphously perverse child to become a properly functioning, non-incestuous, reproductive heterosexual adult. For Lacan, desire is "the desire of the Other;" desire is always structured within the phallogocentric Symbolic Order. For both Freud and Lacan, desire is based on the idea of lack or absence, reinforced by the Western cultural insistence on the centrality of a metaphysics of presence.

From a psychoanalytic point of view, humans are scared of lack, especially as symbolized through anatomy: for Freud, the visible presence of the penis was reassuring, in contrast to the frightening dark hole, the nothing, of the female genitalia—the place the penis longs to go, but from which fears it may not ever return. This is what Hélène Cixous mocks in

"The Laugh of the Medusa"—the Medusa is laughing at this trembling fear of lack, of loss. She, with her dreadful snake locks, is full and multiple and more than just "complete," outside the framework of castration anxiety that is part of the grand narrative of psychoanalysis.

The psychoanalytic emphasis on lack creates desire. You always want something more, something that's missing, something that will fill you up and make you feel good. This is the same concept of desire that fuels capitalism, according to Deleuze and Guattari. Capitalism also requires the endless creation of lack, of need, in

Pierre-Félix Guattari

order to create ever new products for ever new markets. The grand narrative of capitalism is endless growth premised on endless need—a perfect parallel to the psychoanalytic story of endless pursuit of something forever lost.

And so, Deleuze and Guattari ask, what other kind of story might be told? What kind of narrative *not* based on lack or loss?

The two theorists argue that the Freudian psychoanalytic model of the unconscious is a form of "representational theater" in which desires are symbolized, then acted out or performed, as in dreams, but censored by the superego from becoming fully conscious. Instead, Deleuze and Guattari posit a "factory model" of desire, following Foucault in arguing that desire, like power/knowledge, is a productive force.

Desire is not about some unconscious maladjustment to body parts or even about language. Desire is mechanistic, and human subjects are "desiring machines." A desiring machine is described in terms of electrical currents, as a circuit breaker in a larger circuit of other machines. A desiring machine produces a flow of desire from itself that circulates among all the other machines to which it is connected, just as their desire flows into and through it. Hence the object of desire for a desiring machine is another desiring machine connected to it.

Deleuze and Guattari's desiring machines are subject positions defined by desire as a productive force rather than as a lack—positions that are always shifting, always producing more. In the logic of capitalism, desiring machines are saying "I want" and "I want more."

Except that in Deleuze and Guattari's postmodern world, there is no "I" or "self," no individuality that distinguishes one desiring machine from another. One machine is identical to all other machines.

Anti-Oedipus also includes a critique of the idea of "the family" enshrined within Freud's and Lacan's portraits of infant development. Freud posited the family as an eternal closed structure, a universal triangle of Mommy-Daddy-Me isolated and insulated from any external or nonfamilial influences.

This holy family has no longer been possible since the advent of television in the 1950s (if it even was possible before). In fact, watching TV is a good model of households as desiring machines—all plugged into the same sets of images, the same models of reality, which they then perform and produce in material practice.

Deleuze and Guattari's model of "family" is that of a unit within productive flows, rather than a biological entity; such a family can consist of any configuration of desiring machines. In that sense, Deleuze and Guattari also critique the compulsory heterosexuality of the Freudian nuclear family. In postmodern culture, sexuality is not limited to, or by, male and female gender roles and heteronormativity. Rather, sexuality is posited as a hundred thousand desiring machines, all connected and all producing multiplicities of flows and surges. This is Medusa's sexuality, as described by Hélène Cixous. Deleuze and Guattari describe it as "molecular sexuality," as opposed to binary "molar sexuality."

Deleuze and Guattari's *A Thousand Plateaus* (1980) is the second part of the work they began with *The Anti-Oedipus*. In it they introduce the concepts of arborescent and rhizomatic modes of thought.

Western philosophy and Western culture, they argue, have always used a particular model of growth as a metaphor for process and progress: the metaphor of a tree. Think of the phrase "great oaks from little acorns grow." In that metaphor, the acorn (the seed) contains within it all the elements necessary for the oak tree to emerge. The acorn is the point of origin, the source, the beginning. The tree grows by continually expanding upward and outward, branching out and spreading vertically. All its leaves and branches point back to their point of origin; all are connected through the acorn that sprouted them.

Arborescence is representative of humanist thought (*remember humanism?*) and the belief that humans—through language, science, and art—can represent or reflect the world. All of Western thought is inherently arborescent, seeking to trace an orderly path, which is always "progress," from a point of origin. An arborescent system is a centered system that imposes hierarchical binary oppositions and everything that follows from that.

Deleuze and Guattari counter the tree model of modern Western thought with the rhizome. A rhizome is a zone of multiplicity where operations and desires flow freely between points. It is a field with no outlines, no particular structure—a field with no center, no governance, no hierarchy.

A **rhizome** is a fungus. Think of the fungus currently growing on your bathroom tile. You can't remove a vital organ and kill it—each part is the same as every other part. If you leave one microbe, it will grow and spread in all directions, without order, without pattern, without individuality or identity—it just grows.

The rhizome is amorphous and "disordered": no acorn, no origin, no tree, no progress; no center, no plot, no direction, no beginning, and no end.

Examples of rhizomes: Potatoes. Crabgrass. The Borg.

And aspen trees. In contrast to oaks, which live as individual units, aspens are collective; they do not grow alone. Rather, the trees in an aspen grove all have a root network in common; individual trees sprout, grow, and die, but the grove itself lives on.

Perhaps the best example of the rhizome is the Internet—zillions of interconnected websites, none of them central, none of them a point of origin or a source. Take out any websites, any search engines, any platforms, and the web still exists. And we, desiring machines, connect ourselves to it at every possible opportunity.

Language is rhizomatic, say Deleuze and Guattari: "A rhizome ceaselessly establishes connections between semiotic chains, organizations of power, and circumstances relative to the arts, sciences, and social struggles . . . there is no language in itself, nor are there any linguistic universals, only a throng of dialects, patois, slangs, and specialized languages." Even what we view as one specific language is composed of multiplicities of languages.

Moreover, they say, we "can analyze language only by decentering it onto other dimensions and other registers. A language is never closed upon itself, except as a function of impotence." In order to analyze language we must look at it rhizomatically, viewing it not simply as language, but as everything related to language. Language is a multiplicity and connects to and encompasses other multiplicities.

In addition to the rhizome, Deleuze and Guattari use the image of a plateau to describe postmodernism. A plateau, they say, is always in the middle; there is always something before and something after. Like a rhizome, a plateau both is always between things, which guarantees its continued growth and existence. The rhizome and plateau cannot return to what precedes them, they always move on, becoming something else.

And so, they conclude, whereas humanism attempts to represent the world and "imposes the verb 'to be,'" the postmodern rhizome continues infinitely with "the conjunction 'and ... and ... and ....'"

FURTHER READING

Essays by individual theorists can be found in a number of anthologies of literary theory. My course, "Introduction to Literary Theory," uses *Literary Theory: An Anthology* (3rd ed., Blackwell, 2004), edited by Julie Rivkin and Michael Ryan. I also recommend *The Norton Anthology of Theory and Criticism* (2nd ed., W.W. Norton, 2010), edited by Vincent Leitch, William Cain, Laurie Finke, Barbara Johnson, John McGowan, T. Denean Sharpley-Whiting, and Jeffrey Williams.

The following works provide good overviews of the field:

Barry, Peter. *Beginning Theory: An Introduction to Literary and Cultural Theory,* 3rd ed. Manchester, UK, and New York: Manchester University Press, 2009.

Bertens, Hans. *Literary Theory: The Basics,* 3rd ed. New York: Routledge, 2014.

Bressler, Charles. *Literary Criticism: An Introduction to Theory and Practice,* 5th ed. Boston: Longman, 2011.

Culler, Jonathan. *Literary Theory: A Very Short Introduction,* 2nd ed. New York: Oxford University Press, 2011.

Eagleton, Terry. *Literary Theory: An Introduction,* 3rd ed. Minneapolis: University of Minnesota Press, 2008.

Hall, Donald. *Literary and Cultural Theory: From Basic Principles to Advanced Applications.* Boston: Houghton Mifflin, 2001.

Klages, Mary. *Key Terms in Literary Theory.* New York: Continuum, 2012.

Klages, Mary. *Literary Theory: A Guide for the Perplexed.* New York: Continuum, 2006.

Ryan, Michael. *Literary Theory: A Practical Introduction,* 2nd ed. Malden, MA: Blackwell, 2007.

Sarup, Madan. *An Introductory Guide to Post-structuralism and Postmodernism,* 2nd ed. Athens: University of Georgia Press, 1993.

Tyson, Lois. *Critical Theory Today: A User-Friendly Guide,* 3rd ed. New York: Routledge, 2014.

There are also many books designed for beginning students that address specific types of theories and provide excellent accessible but not simplistic explanations of the foundations, principles, and problems of each type.

The *For Beginners* series (Danbury, CT) is my personal favorite, of course. These books, in graphic format, are created by knowledgeable teams of writers and illustrators. They make learning theory as fun as reading a comic book or manga novel, and all are accessible and informative (www.forbeginnersbooks.com). Relevant titles in the series include:

Deconstruction For Beginners, by Jim Powell
 (illustrated by Joe Lee)
Derrida For Beginners, by Jim Powell
 (illustrated by Van Howell)
Foucault For Beginners, by Lydia Alix Fillingham
(illustrated by Moshe Susser)
Lacan For Beginners, by Philip Hill
 (illustrated by David Leach)
Linguistics For Beginners, by W. Terrence Gordon
(illustrated by Susan Willmarth)
Marx's Das Kapital For Beginners, by Michael Wayne
(illustrated by Sungyoon Choi)
Nietzsche For Beginners, by Marc Sautet
 (illustrated by Patrick Boussignac)
Philosophy For Beginners, by Richard Osborne
(illustrated by Ralph Edney)
Plato For Beginners, by Robert Cavelier
 (illustrated by Eric Lurio)
Postmodernism For Beginners, by Jim Powell
 (illustrated by Joe Lee)
Saussure For Beginners, by W. Terrence Gordon
(illustrated by Abbe Lubell)
Structuralism and Poststructuralism For Beginners,
 by Donald Palmer

Finally, I recommend looking on YouTube. You'll find many videos of theorists talking about their work, and of professors from various universities offering explanations.

ABOUT THE AUTHOR

Mary Klages is an Associate Professor in the English Department of the University of Colorado at Boulder, where she is notorious for her use of Tinkertoys in the classroom. She is the author of *Literary Theory: A Guide for the Perplexed* (Continuum, 2006) and *Key Terms in Literary Theory* (Continuum, 2012), as well as several scholarly works in the fields of American literary history and Disability Studies. When not occupied by teaching, research, writing, raising two children, and caring for a variety of animals, she enjoys sleeping.

ABOUT THE ILLUSTRATOR

Frank Reynoso is an author and commercial artist based in Brooklyn, New York. His work has appeared in numerous comics including *The Sweetness* (Z2 Comics), *Occupy Comics* (Black Mask Studios), *and World War 3 Illustrated.* He has illustrated *Civil Rights For Beginners* (2016). He enjoys comedy, science fiction, and dark fantasy with wine and good friends.

THE FOR BEGINNERS® SERIES

ABSTRACT EXPRESSIONISM	ISBN 978-1-939994-62-2
AFRICAN HISTORY FOR BEGINNERS	ISBN 978-1-934389-18-8
AMERICAN PRESIDENCY, THE	ISBN 978-1-939994-70-7
ANARCHISM FOR BEGINNERS	ISBN 978-1-934389-32-4
ARABS & ISRAEL FOR BEGINNERS	ISBN 978-1-934389-16-4
ART THEORY FOR BEGINNERS	ISBN 978-1-934389-47-8
ASTRONOMY FOR BEGINNERS	ISBN 978-1-934389-25-6
AYN RAND FOR BEGINNERS	ISBN 978-1-934389-37-9
BARACK OBAMA FOR BEGINNERS, AN ESSENTIAL GUIDE	ISBN 978-1-934389-44-7
BEN FRANKLIN FOR BEGINNERS	ISBN 978-1-934389-48-5
BLACK HISTORY FOR BEGINNERS	ISBN 978-1-934389-19-5
THE BLACK HOLOCAUST FOR BEGINNERS	ISBN 978-1-934389-03-4
BLACK PANTHERS FOR BEGINNERS	ISBN 978-1-939994-39-4
BLACK WOMEN FOR BEGINNERS	ISBN 978-1-934389-20-1
BUDDHA FOR BEGINNERS	ISBN 978-1-939994-33-2
BUKOWSKI FOR BEGINNERS	ISBN 978-1-939994-37-0
CHICANO MOVEMENT FOR BEGINNERS	ISBN 978-1-939994-64-6
CHOMSKY FOR BEGINNERS	ISBN 978-1-934389-17-1
CIVIL RIGHTS FOR BEGINNERS	ISBN 978-1-934389-89-8
CLIMATE CHANGE FOR BEGINNERS	ISBN 978-1-939994-43-1
DADA & SURREALISM FOR BEGINNERS	ISBN 978-1-934389-00-3
DANTE FOR BEGINNERS	ISBN 978-1-934389-67-6
DECONSTRUCTION FOR BEGINNERS	ISBN 978-1-934389-26-3
DEMOCRACY FOR BEGINNERS	ISBN 978-1-934389-36-2
DERRIDA FOR BEGINNERS	ISBN 978-1-934389-11-9
EASTERN PHILOSOPHY FOR BEGINNERS	ISBN 978-1-934389-07-2
EXISTENTIALISM FOR BEGINNERS	ISBN 978-1-934389-21-8
FANON FOR BEGINNERS	ISBN 978-1-934389-87-4
FDR AND THE NEW DEAL FOR BEGINNERS	ISBN 978-1-934389-50-8
FOUCAULT FOR BEGINNERS	ISBN 978-1-934389-12-6
FRENCH REVOLUTIONS FOR BEGINNERS	ISBN 978-1-934389-91-1
GENDER & SEXUALITY FOR BEGINNERS	ISBN 978-1-934389-69-0
GREEK MYTHOLOGY FOR BEGINNERS	ISBN 978-1-934389-83-6
HEIDEGGER FOR BEGINNERS	ISBN 978-1-934389-13-3
THE HISTORY OF CLASSICAL MUSIC FOR BEGINNERS	ISBN 978-1-939994-26-4
THE HISTORY OF OPERA FOR BEGINNERS	ISBN 978-1-934389-79-9
ISLAM FOR BEGINNERS	ISBN 978-1-934389-01-0
JANE AUSTEN FOR BEGINNERS	ISBN 978-1-934389-61-4
JUNG FOR BEGINNERS	ISBN 978-1-934389-76-8
KIERKEGAARD FOR BEGINNERS	ISBN 978-1-934389-14-0
LACAN FOR BEGINNERS	ISBN 978-1-934389-39-3
LIBERTARIANISM FOR BEGINNERS	ISBN 978-1-939994-66-0
LINCOLN FOR BEGINNERS	ISBN 978-1-934389-85-0
LINGUISTICS FOR BEGINNERS	ISBN 978-1-934389-28-7
MALCOLM X FOR BEGINNERS	ISBN 978-1-934389-04-1
MARX'S DAS KAPITAL FOR BEGINNERS	ISBN 978-1-934389-59-1
MCLUHAN FOR BEGINNERS	ISBN 978-1-934389-75-1
MORMONISM FOR BEGINNERS	ISBN 978-1-939994-52-3
MUSIC THEORY FOR BEGINNERS	ISBN 978-1-939994-46-2
NIETZSCHE FOR BEGINNERS	ISBN 978-1-934389-05-8
PAUL ROBESON FOR BEGINNERS	ISBN 978-1-934389-81-2
PHILOSOPHY FOR BEGINNERS	ISBN 978-1-934389-02-7
PLATO FOR BEGINNERS	ISBN 978-1-934389-08-9
POETRY FOR BEGINNERS	ISBN 978-1-934389-46-1
POSTMODERNISM FOR BEGINNERS	ISBN 978-1-934389-09-6
PROUST FOR BEGINNERS	ISBN 978-1-939994-44-8
RELATIVITY & QUANTUM PHYSICS FOR BEGINNERS	ISBN 978-1-934389-42-3
SARTRE FOR BEGINNERS	ISBN 978-1-934389-15-7
SAUSSURE FOR BEGINNERS	ISBN 978-1-939994-41-7
SHAKESPEARE FOR BEGINNERS	ISBN 978-1-934389-29-4
STANISLAVSKI FOR BEGINNERS	ISBN 978-1-939994-35-6
STRUCTURALISM & POSTSTRUCTURALISM FOR BEGINNERS	ISBN 978-1-934389-10-2
TESLA FOR BEGINNERS	ISBN 978-1-939994-48-6
TONI MORRISON FOR BEGINNERS	ISBN 978-1-939994-54-7
WOMEN'S HISTORY FOR BEGINNERS	ISBN 978-1-934389-60-7
UNIONS FOR BEGINNERS	ISBN 978-1-934389-77-5
U.S. CONSTITUTION FOR BEGINNERS	ISBN 978-1-934389-62-1
ZEN FOR BEGINNERS	ISBN 978-1-934389-06-5
ZINN FOR BEGINNERS	ISBN 978-1-934389-40-9